# Seasons
## of Love

### Bride, Warrior, Child, Leading Lady

## GIGI BORROMEO

WestBow
PRESS
A DIVISION OF THOMAS NELSON

WestBow Press books may be ordered through booksellers or by contacting:

WestBow Press
A Division of Thomas Nelson
1663 Liberty Drive
Bloomington, IN 47403
www.westbowpress.com
1 (866) 928-1240

ISBN: 978-1-4908-1642-5 (sc)
ISBN: 978-1-4908-1643-2 (hc)

Library of Congress Control Number: 2013921629

Printed in the United States of America.

WestBow Press rev. date: 12/06/2013

# Contents

# Dedication

**TO MY SAVIOR I SAY: "Here Lord is my loaves and fishes. Bless this work and feed the multitude."**

I dedicate this book to my first pastor, Brother Jack Edward. Brother Edward fought in both World War I and II and has since gone to be with Jesus. Brother Edward laid the foundation of the Gospel for me along with many Sunday School teachers and youth workers.

Secondly, I want to thank and dedicate this book to Pastor Larry Roper, of the Light Ministries Church in Antioch, CA, who taught me many Kingdom principals, was there for the birth of two of my children and never condemned me publicly or otherwise. He was nurturing and loving and will always have a special place in my heart.

Thirdly, I want to dedicate this book to my current pastors, Pastor Pete and Beverly Williams of Freedom Church, Red Bluff, CA, who have revealed the latter revelations of God's word on my spiritual inheritance. You have taken me to a completely new level of hope. Together, they have taught me Kingdom culture, my true identity, my purpose and significance.

Lastly, I want to dedicate this book to my daughters, nieces, cousins, Aunts, and girlfriends - all the women in my life that I love dearly.

# Introduction

I am told that there are over Seven-Thousand promises in God's Word. It's my desire that my love ones know all the promises available to them, and they know the purpose for which they were created for and their created destiny. This is why I included so many scriptures. All scriptures are promises. Whenever, the promises refer to Israel, Judah, Jerusalem or Zion, we can put our name there. We are God's chosen people. If you are not born of Jewish descent you are a Gentile. Because of the Jew's rejection to Jesus, being the King of Kings and Lord of Lords, the Gentiles were adopted into the family of God, so that they too may partake of the good promises of God.

When God's Word speaks of Egypt, it refers to our sin nature, our rebellion and slavery to sin.

**Romans 11:12**

> The world received good things from God because of the sin of the Jews. Because the Jews did not receive God's free gift, the people who are not Jews received good things from Him. Think how much more the world will receive when the Jews finish God's plan by putting their trust in Christ! (NLT)

**Romans 9:4**

They are the people of Israel, chosen to be God's adopted children. God revealed his glory to them. He made covenants with them and gave them his law. He gave them the privilege of worshiping him and receiving his wonderful promises. (NLT)

# THE BRIDE

**Spring** *is in the air, warm temperatures and*
*clear blue skies*
*Buddings of new life dawn the day*
*Newness of life brings on a new scent in the air, warming our soul*
*Senses of new hope and joy splash in our heart*
*So quickly it visits and passes through*
*Come back, Come back, oh joyous Spring!*

# Perfect Love

*"Where do I begin to tell the sweet love story
of how great a love can be. . . . . ."*

Spring is sometimes known for its exciting season of love and romance. It is recorded that there were literally, millions of viewers of the recent Royal Wedding of Prince William and Kate; I being one. Truth be told, I love love-stories. True love is priceless and we either rejoice or envy the beholders of them who have found it.

As a young girl, I dreamed of a time I would wed a handsome young man, just a head taller than me, so that I could look up at him as he spoke. He would tilt his head down to kiss me. Handsome and nice was the only pre-requisite, when I had almost no knowledge of a real intimate relationship. Later, putting aside all the romantic notions, I decided a man who loves God, is strong in character, decisive and full of integrity is the preferred man for me. Since he will lead the home, he must rule decisively, but he must also have a gentler side and sensitive, enough, to express his warm love toward his bride. This perfect man would be one who would share his heart and his deep inner-thoughts. He would need to love passionately and always remain faithful. He would need to be wise, intelligent and discerning. He should love and want many children. He would have good work ethics in order to be an excellent provider. That pretty much sums up the perfect husband in my eyes. Oh, and one more thing, I would not have to go looking for him, he would pursue me; he must lock his eyes on me and claim love at first sight.

The groom is smitten with his bride and the bride adores her groom. Isn't that just about how most of us start out in marriage? He asks for her hand in marriage and she accepts. Then the waiting begins as the preparations are excitingly being made. She chooses her gown, her jewels and the guest whom she will invite to the celebration. Careful consideration, of the details are made because the day is to be as perfect and lovely as possible. Flowers and decorations will adorn her walk as she walks down the isle to her groom. The groom will be there waiting to see the look on his bride's face. Is she nervous, emotional, elated, or will she hide her emotions behind a simple smile? They exchange looks. All guest arise as a show of honor. The music begins and so does the long walk. The walk is slow and for the bride, it seems too slow. She is quite anxious and all eyes are on her. The bride has prepared herself. She has adorned her hair. Her nails are neatly manicured and her cosmetics are applied to enhance her beauty. Everyone enjoys watching the bride because she is in her glory. She is at her most perfect weight and may never return to this size again. The photos taken will remind her of the beauty that surrounds her.

As a parallel, Christ is our most perfect groom; all his attributes are perfect, as he is sinless, whole and complete. This one ancient love-story I'll never tire of, is between Jesus Son of God and his Bride the Church. In Revelation 21:9, the Believers are referred to as the Bride of Christ, and also the Lamb's wife. He chose us, his Bride, out of the world and he pursued us. We, who are "born again," have accepted his gift and entered into the covenant, thereby being bought and purchased, we receive all the benefits of marriage - the blessings, the inheritance and eternal life.

Of course, God is an infinite Spirit, eternal and unchangeable. In his being is wisdom, power, holiness, justice, goodness and truth. Therefore to enter a relationship with him, one must be born of the Spirit and not of the natural. If you have accepted Jesus Christ as your personal Savior you have found the bridegroom of a lifetime and when he returns, there will be a wedding feast.

**Revelation 21:9**

"Come, I will show you the bride, the wife of the lamb." (NIV)

**John 15:9**

I have loved you just as My Father has loved Me. Stay in My love. (NLV)

**John 6:44**

No one can come to me, unless the Father who sent me makes them want to come. But if they do come, I will raise them to life on the last day. (CEV)

**Revelation 19:9**

Then the angel told me, "Put this in writing. God will bless everyone who is invited to the wedding feast of the Lamb." The angel also said, "These things that God has said are true." (CEV)

**John 3:3**

Jesus answered, "I assure you, everyone must be born again. Anyone who is not born again cannot be in God's kingdom." (ERV)

**1 Corinthians 7:23**

> You were bought at a price; do not become slaves of human beings. (NIV)

> Although, it is quite impossible to explore all of His infiniteness, let's look at only some, of his attributes.

## Behold your King, Your Majesty is Smitten in Love

As a king summons his bride, we too are summoned to be with him because, we belong to him. The scriptures tells us how precious and honored we are since he created us and formed us. No one knows us as deeply and intimate as he does. He left his heavenly home and perfect kingdom to redeem us when we were in trouble. When the wages of our sin was required of us, he affirmed his love at the cross of calvary and always to give us the gift of eternal life.

**Matthew 20:28**

> Even as the Son of Man came not to be served but to serve, and to give his life as a ransom for many. (ESV)

**John 3:16**

> God loved the people of this world so much that he gave his only Son, so that everyone who has faith in him will have eternal life and never really die. (CEV)

**Isaiah 43:1**

> But now, God's Message, the God who made you in the first place, Jacob, the One who got you started, Israel: "Don't

be afraid, I've redeemed you. I've called your name. You're mine. When you're in over your head, I'll be there with you. When you're in rough waters, you will not go down. When you're between a rock and a hard place, it won't be a dead end—Because I am God, your personal God, the Holy of Israel, your Savior. I paid a huge price for you. (Message)

**Isaiah 49:16**

Behold, I have graven thee upon the palms of my hands; thy walls are continually before me. (KJV)

In these next two passages, Jeremiah 31:3 and Song of Solomon 2:8-13 we see that the Lord draws us to him by his unfailing kindness. In Deuteronomy 30:19, we are given the choice both of life and death - blessings and curses. The Lord has given us a free will to choose whomever we want to serve. To choose to the King of Kings is to choose life. The Lord, King Jesus is beckoning us to come away with him. In Song of Solomon you hear his gentle plea, like a playful and love-bound pursuer. Choosing the King of Kings will mean blessings of an everlasting love.

**Jeremiah 31:3**

The Lord appeared to him from afar, saying, "I have loved you with an everlasting love; therefore I have drawn you with lovingkindness. (NASB)

**Song of Solomon 2:8-13**

Listen! My beloved! Look! Here he comes, leaping across the mountains, bounding over the hills. My beloved is like a gazelle or a young stag. Look! There he stands behind our wall, gazing through the windows, peering through the lattice. My beloved spoke and said to me, "Arise, my darling, my beautiful one, come with me. See! The winter is past; the rains are over and gone. Flowers appear on the earth; the season of singing has come, the cooing of doves is heard in our land. The fig tree forms its early fruit; the blossoming vines spread their fragrance. Arise, come, my darling; my beautiful one, come with me." (NIV)

**Deuteronomy 30:19-20**

I call heaven and earth as witnesses today against you, that I have set before you life and death, blessing and cursing; therefore choose life, that both you and your descendants may live; that you may love the Lord your God, that you may obey His voice, and that you may cling to Him, for He is your life and the length of your days; and that you may dwell in the land which the Lord swore to your fathers, to Abraham, Isaac, and Jacob, to give them." (NKJV)

**Matthew 16:25**

For whosoever will save his life shall lose it: and whosoever will lose his life for my sake shall find it. (KJV)

In chapter 1 of Song of Solomon, the young maiden knew in her heart that she could never measure up in comparison to her perfect king, who is a prophetic depiction of Christ. The maiden had realized her blackness (sin) and inadequacy; she said, "I am black but comely." Despite this, the maiden knew that she was loved by the King (Song of Solomon 1:5). Christ our king, loved us so much that while we were yet in our sins, he laid down his life for us to redeem us to himself. Since then, he holds the scars in his hands to remind us that nothing will ever separate us from his love. We now bear his name and are made right and clean through his righteousness and redemption.

**Romans 5:8**

> But God demonstrates his own love for us in this: While we were still sinners, Christ died for us. (NIV)

**Romans 8:38-39**

> I am sure that nothing can separate us from God's love— not life or death, not angels or spirits, not the present or the future, and not powers above or powers below. Nothing in all creation can separate us from God's love for us in Christ Jesus our Lord! (CEV)

## Behold your King is Faithful

Because the Lord Jesus is holy and righteous he is faithful to eternity. Unlike many marriages in this temporal life, marriage between Jesus Christ our King, and us his bride, will last throughout eternity. We can be confident that, although we are not yet perfect and occasionally "burn the toast," so to speak, the Lord Jesus is at work each day to prepare us for our heavenly home. We will learn how to stand confidently.

**Deuteronomy 32:4**

> He's the Rock, and His work is perfect; everything He does is right. He's the God who can be trusted, who never does wrong because He's righteous and upright. (VOICE)

**Hosea 2:20**

> And I will betroth you to Me in faithfulness. Then you will know the Lord. (NASB)

**Psalm 57:10**

> Your love reaches higher than the heavens; your loyalty extends beyond the clouds. (CEV)

**Psalm 86:15**

> But you, O Lord, are a God of compassion and mercy, slow to get angry and filled with unfailing love and faithfulness. (NLT)

**Philippians 1:6**

> Being confident of this very thing, that He who has begun a good work in you will complete it until the day of Jesus Christ; (NKJV)

Contrary to the Lord's divine role of leadership, Esau cared very little for leadership and sold his birthright (Gen. 25:32). Without any vision or direction from our Divine Savior, many husbands have relinquished there God-given right to spiritually lead their families. As a result, many wives have stepped into the role to lead, but unfortunately to the shame of their husbands.

## Behold your King is Strong and Powerful

King Jesus, is a strong ruler who knows how to rule decisively. He will not lead us astray. Jesus Christ is the same yesterday, today and forever and completely unchangeable (Hebrews 13:8). What he purposes to do he will indeed do it (Is. 46:11). Although heaven and earth will pass away, his words will by no means pass away (Matthew 24:35). When someone actually means what they say and says what they mean, you can put your solid trust in them. The Lord can be trusted. He is a mighty rock and rules with a mighty hand so that we lack nothing. The Lord's throne cannot be overthrown. His throne is secure because it is established in love.

**Ephesians 1:21**

God has put Christ over all rulers, authorities, powers, and kings, not only in this world but also in the next. (NCV)

**Isaiah 16:5**

In love a throne will be established; in faithfulness a man will sit on it—one from the house of David— one who in judging seeks justice and speeds the cause of righteousness. (NIV)

**Deuteronomy 3:24**

Lord God, you have begun to show me, your servant, how great you are. You have great strength, and no other god in heaven or on earth can do the powerful things you do. There is no other god like you. (NCV)

**Deuteronomy 4:34**

Or has any god ever tried to take one nation out of another nation using tests, miracles, wonders, war, a strong hand and outstretched arm, or awesome power like all that the Lord your God did for you in Egypt while you watched? (CEB)

**Deuteronomy 5:15**

Remember that you were slaves in Egypt and that the Lord your God brought you out of there by his great power and strength. So the Lord your God has commanded you to rest on the Sabbath day. (NCV)

**Psalm 96:9**

Worship the Lord in all his holy beauty. Everyone on earth should tremble before him. (ERV)

## Behold your King is Gentle

While King Jesus rules with strength and power, he is also, gentle as a shepherd with his lambs. He is ready to gather you in his arms in order to give you rest. He humbles himself in obedience to the father to give you a complete and abundant life. He cares for you and will never change his heart for you. He is a covenant maker and he is good and he is kind. He will carry your deepest hurts in order to take up the heaviness of your heart.

**Isaiah 40:11**

He will feed His flock like a shepherd; He will gather the lambs with His arm, and carry them in His bosom, And gently lead those who are with young. (NKJV)

**Revelation 7:17**

For the Lamb in the midst of the throne will be their shepherd, and he will guide them to springs of living water, and God will wipe away every tear from their eyes." (ESV)

**Deuteronomy 33:12**

"Let the beloved of the LORD rest secure in him, for he shields him all day long, and the one the LORD loves rests between his shoulders." (NIV)

**Matthew 11:29**

Accept my teachings and learn from me, because I am gentle and humble in spirit, and you will find rest for your lives. (NCV)

**Philippians 2:8**

And being found in human form, he humbled himself by becoming obedient to the point of death, even death on a cross. (ESV)

## Behold Your King Is Wealthy

King Jesus owns everything. He does indeed bless us materially, but not without purpose. It is not to squander those resources on ourselves, but to be good stewards, using our resources wisely so as to win the lost and bring them to the Lord Jesus Christ.

**Deuteronomy 15:4**

But there will be no poor among you; for the Lord will bless you in the land that the Lord your God is giving you for an inheritance to possess— (ESV)

**1 Peter 4:10**

> Each of you has been blessed with one of God's many wonderful gifts to be used in the service of others. So use your gift well. (CEV)

**Psalm 50:10**

> I already own all the animals in the forest. I own all the animals on a thousand hills. (ERV)

**2 Chronicles 1:12**

> Therefore wisdom and knowledge will be given you. And I will also give you wealth, riches and honor, such as no king who was before you ever had and none after you will have." (NIV)

**Psalm 112:3**

> Wealth and riches will be in his house, and his righteousness endures forever. (NKJV)

**Nehemiah 9:6**

> You are the only Lord. You made the heavens, even the highest heavens, with all the stars. You made the earth and everything on it, the seas and everything in them; you give life to everything. The heavenly army worships you. (NCV)

**Proverbs 8:21**

> I give wealth to those who love me, filling their houses with treasures. (NEC)

**Exodus 19:5**

. Now if you will obey me and keep my covenant, you will be my own special treasure from among all the peoples on earth; for all the earth belongs to me. (NLT)

## Behold Your King Is Wise

He who understands the heavens and the earth and who formed you in your mother's womb, can surely understand your needs and counsel you by his rich wisdom. We can be secure in him who has all wisdom, knowledge, and power and knows what is best for us. He can guide you to invest your life in worthwhile ways. As you bask in the knowledge of his words, you will discover the riches of wisdom as you walk with him and listen to him. He will provide guidance for your crooked ways.

**Proverbs 2:6-8**

For the LORD gives wisdom, and from his mouth come knowledge and understanding. He holds victory in store for the upright, he is a shield to those whose walk is blameless, for he guards the course of the just and protects the way of his faithful ones. (NIV)

**2 Chronicles 1:10**

Give me wisdom and knowledge so I can lead this people, because no one can govern this great people of yours without your help." (CEB)

**1 Kings 4:29**

> And God gave Solomon wisdom and understanding beyond measure, and breadth of mind like the sand on the seashore. (ESV)

**2 Chronicles 1:12**

> So I will make you wise and intelligent. But I will also make you richer and more famous than any king before or after you. (CEV)

**Isaiah 44:24**

> This is what the Lord says—your Redeemer and Creator: "I am the Lord, who made all things. I alone stretched out the heavens. (NLT)

**Daniel 2:20**

> He reveals deep and secret things; He knows what is in the darkness, And light dwells with Him. (NKJV)

**Psalm 139:4**

> You know what I'm going to say long before I say it. It is true, Eternal One, that You know everything and everyone. (VOICE)

# You are Chosen

This then is his love story, that he, the King of Kings and Savior of the world, knows you, seeks you, chose you, courts you, died to redeemed you to him, protects you and then rewards you with the riches of his love forever. He is the perfect groom and the lover of all souls! The bridegroom is entirely smitten by you and rejoices over you.

Do you not feel like Queen Ester, who was chosen among all the beautiful maidens of the country? Yet, we did not look for him. He first loved us and we were gently drawn unto him by his sweet and gentle spirit. You Brides were chosen from out of the world. Do you realize we could not have known God except that he chose to make himself known to us? God wants us to know him because he has created us for a personal and intimate relationship with himself.

**Jeremiah 1:5**

> "Before I made you in your mother's womb, I knew you.
> Before you were born, I chose you for a special work. I chose
> you to be a prophet to the nations." (ERV)

**John 15:16**

You did not choose me, but I chose you and appointed you so that you might go and bear fruit – fruit that will last. (NIV)

**John 14:6**

Jesus said to him, "I am the way, and the truth, and the life. No one comes to the Father except through me. (ESV)

**Deuteronomy 7:6**

For you are a holy people to the Lord your God; the Lord your God has chosen you to be a people for his own possession out of all the peoples who are on the face of the earth. (NASB)

**Psalm 65:4**

How blessed is the one whom You choose and bring near to You to dwell in Your courts. We will be satisfied with the goodness of Your house, Your holy temple. (NASB)

**Ephesians 5:26-27**

Christ loved the church and gave himself up for her to make her holy, cleansing her by the washing with water through the word, and to present her to himself as a radiant church, without stain or wrinkle or any other blemish, but holy and blameless. (NIV)

**Isaiah 62:4**

Never again will you be called "The Forsaken City" or "The Desolate Land." Your new name will be "The City of God's Delight" and "The Bride of God," for the LORD delights in you and will claim you as his bride. (NLT)

# The Inheritance

Because you have accepted your groom's hand in marriage, you have entered a covenant relationship and will forever be blessed. It is simply God's nature and character to love and bless. For what has he withheld from us? After choosing us and giving us redemption through his blood, which is no small price, he then gives us every blessing in the heavenly realms (Ephesians 1:3). Psalm 23:6, reads: "Surely goodness and mercy shall follow me all the days of my life and I will dwell in the house of the LORD forever." We only hear about the *forevers* in fairytales, but will you dare to believe that this is what the Lord and King offers you because he is an eternal, loving God. Psalm 103, reminds us not to forget all his benefits. We must hold on to these truths because our enemy wants for us to forget the promises of God and become crippled. Once crippled, lame and weak he hopes to render us ineffective in the Lord's kingdom. When we choose not to believe in the promises of our King and believe in the lies of the Accuser we separate ourselves from our groom.

Even still when we fail him miserably, if we would continually believe in him, he would turn our mourning into dancing, curses into blessings, sorrow into gladness and give us a spirit of praise, instead of sadness. He desires to build us up to become a victorious and glorious bride. Oh, what promises he gives to us! Will you believe, Bride of Christ? All that the groom does is to benefit us, because he is a wellspring of life!

**Isaiah 54:5**

> For your Creator will be your husband; (NLT)

**Matthew 25:34**

> Then the King will say to those on His right hand, 'Come, you blessed of My Father, inherit the kingdom prepared for you from the foundation of the world. (NKJV)

**Psalm 103:1-2**

> Bless the Lord, O my soul, and all that is within me, bless His holy name. Bless the Lord, O my soul, and forget none of His benefits; who pardons all your iniquities, who heals all your diseases; (NASB)

**Matthew 8:17**

> This fulfilled the word of the Lord through the prophet Isaiah, who said, "He took our sicknesses and removed our diseases." (NLT)

**Deuteronomy 23:5**

> But the Lord your God refused to do what Balaam asked. Instead, the Lord changed the curse into a blessing for you, because the Lord your God loves you. (ERV)

**Isaiah 61:3**

> He wants me to help those in Zion who are filled with sorrow. I will put beautiful crowns on their heads in place of ashes. I will anoint them with oil to give them gladness instead of sorrow. I will give them a spirit of praise in place of a spirit of sadness. They will be like oak trees that are strong and straight. The Lord himself will plant them in the land. That will show how glorious he is. (NIV)

**Ecclesiastes 3:11**

> God makes everything happen at the right time. Yet none of us can ever fully understand all he has done, and he puts questions in our minds about the past and the future. (CEV)

For any relationship to exist, those involved must share some knowledge of each other. The more intimate the knowledge, the more personal the relationship becomes. God knows you to the smallest detail of your life - things you couldn't even know about yourself, he knows. The realization that God loves you can satisfy your basic need for self-worth. Consider the sense of worth you might experience should you discover that you are cherished and loved. You are loved by the King of Kings and Lord of Lords, the Creator of all things - the One of whom the Scriptures declares. That's amazing love!

**Luke 12:7**

> But even the very hairs of your head are all numbered. Fear not therefore: ye are of more value than many sparrows. (KJV)

**Psalm 56:8**

You have kept record of my days of wandering. You have stored my tears in your bottle and counted each of them. (CEV)

**Matthew 6:8**

Don't be like them, because your Father knows what you need before you ask. (CEB)

# Responding to His Love

Because true love will always erect a response, the bride will prepare herself in response to the groom's love for her. She will clothe herself in his righteousness. She will run away with him to live the full adventure of knowing and doing the will of God. She will submit to her King and obey his commands, fully trusting in his every word as an expression of her love. She will incline her ear to hear him. She will patiently wait upon her King for instructions. She will join him where he leads. She will love him with all her heart, all her soul, with all her mind and with every bit of her strength. She will pursue his will and not her own, and she will desire his will, above all else. It is our deepest need to belong, to be in a relationship and to have a spiritual and emotional home.

Therefore, he will build her a home and she will lay up her treasures, where her mind will be at peace and she will know rest.

**Isaiah 61:10**

> I will sing for joy in God, explode in praise from deep in my soul! He dressed me up in a suit of salvation, he outfitted me in a robe of righteousness. As a bridegroom who puts on a tuxedo, and a bride a jeweled tiara. For as the earth

bursts with spring wildflowers, and as a garden cascades with blossoms, So the Master, God, brings righteousness into full bloom and puts praise on display before the nations. (MSG)

**Revelation 19:7-9**

Let us rejoice and be happy and give God glory, because the wedding of the Lamb has come, and the Lamb's bride has made herself ready. Fine linen, bright and clean, was given to her to wear." (The fine linen means the good things done by God's holy people.) And the angel said to me, "Write this: Blessed are those who have been invited to the wedding meal of the Lamb!" And the angel said, "These are the true words of God." (NCV)

**John 3:29**

The groom is the one who is getting married. The friend of the groom stands close by and, when he hears him, is overjoyed at the groom's voice. Therefore, my joy is now complete. (CEB)

**Isaiah 62:5**

Your people will take the land, just as a young man takes a bride. The Lord will be pleased because of you, just as a husband is pleased with his bride. (CEV)

**Mark 12:30**

And you shall love the Lord your God out of and with your whole heart and out of and with all your soul (your life) and out of and with all your mind (with your faculty of thought and your moral understanding) and out of and with all your strength. This is the first and principal commandment. (AMP)

**1 Chronicles 28:9**

My son Solomon, always remember the God of your father. Serve him with all your heart. Do it with a mind that wants to obey him. The Lord looks deep down inside every heart. He understands the real reasons for everything you think. If you look to him, you will find him. But if you desert him, he will turn his back on you forever. (NIV)

**Ephesians 2:10**

For we are God's masterpiece. He has created us anew in Christ Jesus, so we can do the good things he planned for us long ago. (NLT)

# Weariness

A bride is typically considered a newlywed for the first couple of years of marriage. While the bride is fresh and newly in love with the Lord, it is not too hard to love the Lord; for the Lord is good. The bride desires to please the Lord. She strives to be pure, holy and righteous. She is a peacemaker. She is faithful to her church, her family and the ministries the Lord has called her to. She is faithful to prayer. She is passionate about her relationship with the Lord. She is sensitive to the Holy Spirit and she joins herself in the things that the Lord is involved with - working side-by-side with him. She looks to him for daily wisdom, guidance and provision.

**Psalm 34:8**

> Taste and see how good the Lord is! The one who takes refuge in him is truly happy! (CEB)

**1 Thessalonians 3:7-8**

> So, brothers and sisters, we are encouraged about you because of your faith. We have much trouble and suffering, but still

we are encouraged. Our life is really full if you stand strong in the Lord. (ERV)

**Galatians 5:6**

The only thing that counts is faith expressing itself through love. (NIV)

**1 Thessalonians 4:11-12**

And to make it your ambition to lead a quiet life and attend to your own business and work with your hands, just as we commanded you, so that you will behave properly toward outsiders and not be in any need. (NASB)

**Matthew 25:21**

"His master replied, 'Well done, good and faithful servant! You have been faithful with a few things; I will put you in charge of many things. Come and share your master's happiness!' (NIV)

**1 Peter 1:16**

It is written, You will be holy, because I am holy. (CEB)

**Philippians 2:5-8**

Your attitude should be the same as that of Christ Jesus: Who, being in very nature God, did not consider equality with God something to be grasped, but made himself nothing, taking the very nature of a servant, being made in human likeness. And being found in appearance as a man, he humbled himself and became obedient to death — even death on a cross! (NIV 1984)

**Proverbs 3:5-6**

With all your heart you must trust the Lord and not your own judgment. Always let him lead you, and he will clear the road for you to follow. (CEV)

At some point in the bride's life, when the romance begins to fade, a false reality begins to set in for the bride that she is simply coping with life. The bride often longs for the euphoria of yesteryear. Even though we are destined for heaven, this world is not our home. It is merely our temporal home and the reality is there are a lot of problems with our temporal home. The bride finds herself constantly working and striving to be good enough to get into God's good grace. This concept however is a fallacy, since we were not saved by works but by grace alone.

Consequently, the bride slowly becomes burdened, weary and worn-out, as she fears she can never measure up to her Lord's standards. Somehow she forgot that she had been chosen and saved by grace - an unearned favor.

**2 Corinthians 1:8-9**

We were under great pressure, far beyond our ability to endure, so that we despaired of life itself. Indeed, we felt we had received the sentence of death. But this happened that we might not rely on ourselves but on God, who raises the dead. (NIV)

**Matthew 25:1-5**

Then the Kingdom of Heaven will be like ten bridesmaids who took their lamps and went to meet the bridegroom. Five of them were foolish, and five were wise. The five who were foolish didn't take enough olive oil for their lamps, but the other five were wise enough to take along extra oil. When the bridegroom was delayed, they all became drowsy and fell asleep. (NLT)

**Matthew 25:6-8**

But at midnight there was a cry, 'Look, the groom! Come out to meet him.' "Then all those bridesmaids got up and prepared their lamps. But the foolish bridesmaids said to the wise ones, 'Give us some of your oil, because our lamps have gone out.' (CEV)

**Ephesians 2:4**

Though we were spiritually dead because of the things we did against God, he gave us new life with Christ. You have been saved by God's grace. (NCV)

We have a tendency to get frustrated by the faults of others - even those we love. We become critical and judgmental of others for their faults. We would rather spin our wheels trying to change others than look at our own hypocrisy; to 'take the log out of our own eye.' We take offense and withdraw love. But if we understood that all souls are truly the Lord's workmanship and not our own, we would be willing to heap more grace upon others, rather than our, often harsh, judgmental attitudes.

More frustrating, is we want immediate relief from our circumstances. We often get impatient waiting on the Lord. It is easier to focus on our eternal home, rather than the reality of this current one. Weariness of waiting on the Lord brings the bride fatigue. The delay causes the bride to slumber.

**Romans 15:5**

> Now may the God who gives the power of patient endurance
> (steadfastness) and who supplies encouragement, grant you
> to live in such mutual harmony *and* such full sympathy with
> one another, in accord with Christ Jesus. (AMP)

**Colossians 3:13**

> Be tolerant with each other and, if someone has a complaint
> against anyone, forgive each other. As the Lord forgave you,
> so also forgive each other. (CEB)

**Luke 6:41**

> You can see the speck in your friend's eye. But you don't
> notice the log in your own eye. (CEV)

**Ephesians 2:10**

> For we are His workmanship, created in Christ Jesus for
> good works, which God prepared beforehand that we should
> walk in them. (NKJV)

For this reason, we will use either of these two coping mechanisms
- "fight" or "flight." We could either fight these desperate thoughts by
using the word of God to get back to salvation by grace, or we could
take flight, by passing up the opportunities to bask in God's word for
more direction, counsel and insight. The ultimate result of "flight" is
unfaithfulness and the result of "fight" is faithfulness. Let's look at what
could be the result of each choice.

Remember Jonah fled from God, not wanting to minister in
Nineveh, a wicked nation, and Jonah was swallowed by the whale,
only to be vomited back, right where God wanted him (Jonah 2:10)?

Remember the prodigal son who left his father's house to galavant in the city, squandering all his inheritance until he was left with no money, home or family and a miserable job, feeding pigs (Luke 15:11-32)? Remember Eli's wicked sons, who had no respect for the Lord or their duties as priest, when they treated the Lord's offerings with contempt (1 Samuel 2:12-13). Eli's son's were disqualified for the ministry and their bloodline would never serve as priest again (1 Samuel 2:30-31).

In fact, the whole ancient world was not spared when God destroyed the whole world of ungodly people with the flood, except for Noah's family (Gen. 6:11-13,17-18).

Consequently, the result of running from God, not honoring the Lord, despising authority, doubting his promises and not spending time with him is rebellion and sin. The tragic result of sin is death. Yet since we have been redeemed from death, the bride is plagued with sorrow, by living beneath the promises of God - sorrow, that ought to lead her back to God.

**Romans 6:23**

> For the wages of sin is death, but the gift of God is eternal life in Christ Jesus our Lord. (NLT)

**1 Samuel 15:23**

> For rebellion is as the sin of witchcraft, And stubbornness is as iniquity and idolatry. Because you have rejected the word of the LORD, He also has rejected you from being king." (NKJV)

**Romans 6:16**

> Surely you know that you become the slaves of whatever you give yourselves to. Anything or anyone you follow will be your master. You can follow sin, or you can obey God.

Following sin brings spiritual death, but obeying God makes you right with him. (ERV)

**Titus 1:16**

They claim to know God, but they deny God by the things that they do. They are detestable, disobedient, and disqualified to do anything good. (CEB)

**2 Corinthians 7:10**

The kind of sorrow God wants makes people decide to change their lives. This leads them to salvation, and we cannot be sorry for that. But the kind of sorrow the world has will bring death. (NCV)

Without faith it is impossible to please God. Since this is true, we need to learn to walk by pure faith and not depend on our emotional feelings. The emotions are a lovely thing, as the Lord God has created them, but because of the *fall*, our emotions are deceitful and cannot be relied on. Emotions can be unpredictable, flighty and unstable. In fact, there is no one, except God, where we can believe one-hundred percent in his character and his promises.

Faith will result in patience and character and ultimately, effectual faith will produce good works. No person who truly has faith in Christ, will not perform good works. Good works are a mark of true Christianity (Matt. 7:20). We grow more intimate with God as we take our relationship with the Lord deeper, by honoring him as we step out in faith and believe his word and his promises. Faith will not always come easily, it is for this reason, that the scripture tells us to fight the good fight of faith.

**Jeremiah 17:9**

> The heart is deceitful above all things. And beyond cure.
> Who can understand it? (NIV)

**Hebrews 10:36**

> For you have need of endurance, so that after you have done
> the will of God, you may receive the promise: (NKJV)

**Hebrews 11:6**

> And without faith it is impossible to please him, for whoever
> would draw near to God must believe that he exists and that
> he rewards those who seek him. (ESV)

**2 Timothy 4:7**

> I have fought well. I have finished the race and I have been
> faithful. (CEV)

The enemies of Christ are constantly trying to steal our faith, our joy and our peace. If our enemies succeed, then we the Bride of Christ, no longer shine like the stars among the people of the world. The world will know that we believe in him when we demonstrate our faith by literally walking in his way. Those who genuinely walk by his precepts are rewarded richly.

**John 10:10**

> A thief comes to steal, kill, and destroy. But I came to give
> life—life that is full and good. (ERV)

**Philippians 2:15**

That you may be blameless and innocent, children of God without blemish in the midst of a crooked and twisted generation, among whom you shine as lights in the world. (ESV)

**Proverbs 12:4**

A wife of noble character is her husband's crown, but a disgraceful wife is like decay in his bones. (NIV)

# Rejected King

Because the world hated our Savior and King and did not receive him as their king, they who are of the world have likewise also hated the Bride. They plotted to have him killed and had him hung on a cross. But because he is the Beginning and the End, the First and the Last and Eternal King, he had devised a plan since the beginning of the world. He died that all might be saved. Comforting us with his Holy Spirit, he returned from whence he came. There in heaven, at the right hand of the Father he prepared a place for us. His promise is that he is coming back again to take us, his Bride home to live with him forevermore.

Most assuredly, the King is coming again!

**John 1:10**

> He was in the world, and though the world was made through him, the world did not recognize him. (NIV)

**John 17:14**

I have given them your teaching. And the world has hated them, because they don't belong to the world, just as I don't belong to the world. (ERV)

**1 Thessalonians 2:15**

Who killed both the Lord Jesus and the prophets, and drove us out, and displease God and oppose all mankind. (ESV)

**Matthew 10:22**

Everyone will hate you on account of my name. But whoever stands firm until the end will be saved. (CEB)

**Acts 5:30**

The God of our fathers raised up Jesus, whom you had put to death by hanging Him on a cross. (NASB)

**Colossians 1:21-23**

At one time you were separated from God. You were his enemies in your minds, and the evil things you did were against God. But now God has made you his friends again. He did this through Christ's death in the body so that he might bring you into God's presence as people who are holy, with no wrong, and with nothing of which God can judge you guilty. This will happen if you continue strong and sure in your faith. You must not be moved away from the hope brought to you by the Good News that you heard. That same Good News has been told to everyone in the world, and I, Paul, help in preaching that Good News. (NCV)

**Acts 14:17**

Nevertheless He did not leave Himself without witness, in that He did good, gave us rain from heaven and fruitful seasons, filling our hearts with food and gladness." (NKJV)

**John 14:1-5**

Do not let your heart be troubled; believe in God, believe also in Me. In My Father's house are many dwelling places; if it were not so, I would have told you; for I go to prepare a place for you. If I go and prepare a place for you, I will come again and receive you to Myself, that where I am, there you may be also. And you know the way where I am going." (NASB)

# *Awaiting the King*

While we are awaiting the coming of our savior and king, he has made these two request of us: to love one another and to make disciples. When he returns, it is recorded in Revelations 4:10, that the elders around the throne will lay their crown at the foot of Jesus and worship him. Both the apostle Paul and apostle James tell us we will be rewarded with a crown of life.

So let us then, not be weary or give up waiting, or compromise our faith. Faith walking should be a regular and passionate part of our Christian walk or else we will eventually abandon it and our life with Christ will suffer loss. The enemy does not abandon his war against the Bride of Christ, although, the tragedy is that many of brides have abandoned their faith and do not remain faithful to Him - to the end.

**Matthew 22:36-40**

> "Teacher, which is the most important commandment in the law of Moses?"

> Jesus replied, "'You must love the Lord your God with all your heart, all your soul, and all your mind.' This is

the first and greatest commandment. A second is equally important: 'Love your neighbor as yourself.' The entire law and all the demands of the prophets are based on these two commandments." (NLT)

**2 Peter 1:5-11**

For this very reason, make every effort to add to your faith goodness; and to goodness knowledge; and to knowledge, self-control; and to self-control, perseverance; and to perseverance, godliness; and to godliness, mutual affection; and to mutual affection, love. For if you possess these qualities in increasing measure, they will keep you from being ineffective and unproductive in your knowledge of our Lord Jesus Christ. But whoever does not have them is nearsighted and blind, forgetting that they have been cleansed from their past sins. Therefore, my brothers and sisters, make every effort to confirm your calling and election. For if you do these things, you will never stumble, and you will receive a rich welcome into the eternal kingdom of our Lord and Savior Jesus Christ. (NIV)

**2 Peter 3:3-4**

It is important for you to understand what will happen in the last days. People will laugh at you. They will live following the evil they want to do. They will say, "Jesus promised to come again. Where is he? Our fathers have died, but the world continues the way it has been since it was made." (ERV)

**Matthew 7:18-22**

A healthy tree cannot bear bad fruit, nor can a diseased tree bear good fruit. Every tree that does not bear good fruit is cut down and thrown into the fire. Thus you will recognize them by their fruits. (ESV)

**John 6:66**

After this, many of His disciples drew back (returned to their old associations) and no longer accompanied Him. (AMP)

# Doubt, Disbelief, Discontent

Where once the Bride wore her inner beauty as a shiny garment, she is now plagued with weariness and sadness. The opposite of peace is fear. Faithlessness leaves us fearful, empty and lonely. When we are wearing fear for a garment, what are we saying about the Lord's care for his bride? When we complain, what are we saying about God's blessings and care for us? Is God who he says he is? Galatians 6:9, warns us not to be weary in doing good, for at the opportune time we will reap the benefits if only we do not lose heart. Just as faithfulness pleases the Lord, unfaithfulness displeases the Lord.

**Galatians 5:7**

> You were running a good race. Who cut in on you to keep you from obeying the truth? (NIV)

**Galatians 5:17**

> The sinful nature wants to do evil, which is just the opposite of what the Spirit wants. And the Spirit gives us desires that are the opposite of what the sinful nature desires. These two

forces are constantly fighting each other, so you are not free to carry out your good intentions. (NLT)

**Ephesians 2:1-3**

At one time you were like a dead person because of the things you did wrong and your offenses against God. You used to act like most people in our world do. You followed the rule of a destructive spiritual power. This is the spirit of disobedience to God's will that is now at work in persons whose lives are characterized by disobedience. At one time you were like those persons. All of you used to do whatever felt good and whatever you thought you wanted so that you were children headed for punishment just like everyone else. (CEB)

**Galatians 6:8-9**

If you follow your selfish desires, you will harvest destruction, but if you follow the Spirit, you will harvest eternal life. Don't get tired of helping others. You will be rewarded when the time is right, if you don't give up. (CEV)

# Abandonment

The Lord came to liberate us from sin. He came to open our eyes so that we turn from darkness to light and from the power of Satan to God. Our King Jesus has purchased our freedom with his blood and forgiven all our sins (Col. 1:13). He gave his life for our ransom so that we could escape eternal punishment and have everlasting life instead. After knowing him and then, abandoning his love and wisdom, we turn our hearts back on all that he has done for us, as though we loved our captivity - this is unfaithfulness.

**Hebrews 4:14**

> Since we have a great high priest, Jesus the Son of God, who has gone into heaven, let us hold on to the faith we have. (NCV)

**1 Timothy 4:1**

> The Spirit clearly says that in the last times some will turn away from what we believe. They will obey spirits that tell lies. And they will follow the teachings of demons. (ERV)

Many of homes our broken and torn apart by unfaithfulness. Lives are ruined and in despair. Unfaithfulness will always bring sorrow to our relationship and intimacy will be destroyed, so it is with our relationship with the Lord Jesus. While obedience and faithfulness means rest, disobedience and unfaithfulness brings turmoil and suffering to our lives, caused by unconfessed sin.

**Ezekiel 16:32**

> You unfaithful wife! You would rather be with strangers than with your own husband! (NIV)

**Psalm 78:8**

> And that they should not be like their fathers, a stubborn and rebellious generation, a generation whose heart was not steadfast, whose spirit was not faithful to God. (ESV)

**Luke 9:62**

> But Jesus said to him, "No one, having put his hand to the plow, and looking back, is fit for the kingdom of God." (NKJV)

**Psalm 78:17-22**

> Yet they still continued to sin against Him, to rebel against the Most High in the desert. And in their heart they put God to the test by asking food according to their desire. Then they spoke against God; they said, "Can God prepare a table in the wilderness? "Behold, He struck the rock so that waters gushed out, and streams were overflowing; can He give bread also? Will He provide meat for His people?" Therefore the Lord heard and was full of wrath; and a fire

was kindled against Jacob and anger also mounted against Israel, because they did not believe in God and did not trust in His salvation. (NASB)

**Isaiah 47:7-8, 10**

You said, 'I will reign forever as queen of the world!' You did not reflect on your actions or think about their consequences. "Listen to this, you pleasure-loving kingdom, living at ease and feeling secure......."You felt secure in your wickedness. 'No one sees me,' you said. But your 'wisdom' and 'knowledge' have led you astray, and you said, 'I am the only one, and there is no other.' (NLT)

**Jeremiah 3:6**

Have you not learned anything from Israel's unfaithful ways? How she turned away from Me, went up every high hill and under every green tree to worship another. She acted like a prostitute and broke our covenant there. (VOICE)

**Jeremiah 3:7-9**

I thought, 'After she has done all this, she will return to me.' But she did not return, and her faithless sister Judah saw this. She saw that I divorced faithless Israel because of her adultery. But that treacherous sister Judah had no fear, and now she, too, has left me and given herself to prostitution. Israel treated it all so lightly—she thought nothing of committing adultery by worshiping idols made of wood and stone. So now the land has been polluted. (NLT)

**Ezekiel 6:9**

Then those of you who escape will remember me among the nations where they are carried captive, how I have been broken over their whoring heart that has departed from me and over their eyes that go whoring after their idols. And they will be loathsome in their own sight for the evils that they have committed, for all their abominations. (ESV)

**Matthew 25:10**

And while they went to buy, the bridegroom came, and those who were ready went in with him to the wedding; and the door was shut. (NKJV)

**Numbers 14:23-24**

This particular generation will never get to enjoy the land I promised to their ancestors so long ago. Although they witnessed My glory and signs firsthand, and the amazing feats I accomplished on their behalf in Egypt and on this desert sojourn, they tested Me over and over again, even 10 times, and even directly disobeyed. None of the people who have turned their backs on Me will ever see the land. For Caleb, though, it's a different matter. He's distinct from the others by having a different spirit and has followed My lead wholeheartedly. I will make sure that he is able to enter the land and to live in it—he and his descendants after him. (VOICE)

**Deuteronomy 28:64-66**

And the Lord will scatter you among all peoples, from one end of the earth to the other; and there you shall serve other gods, of wood and stone, which neither you nor your fathers have known. And among these nations you shall find no ease, and there shall be no rest for the sole of your foot; but the Lord will give you there a trembling heart, and failing eyes, and a languishing soul; your life shall hang in doubt before you; night and day you shall be in dread, and have no assurance of your life. (RSV)

# Restore and Rebuild

The Lord tender in mercy, longs to restore and rebuild your broken ways, along with anything the enemy has stolen from your life. God is always ready for us to repent and begin again. There is no problem our Lord Jesus can not handle. His arms are held open wide, waiting to restore you with the joy of His salvation. The Lord is in the business of restoring relationships. He will not ever turn away a broken and repentant heart. His love never ceases and His mercies are new every morning.

**Ezekiel 11:19**

> Then I will give them one heart, and I will put a new spirit within them, and take the stony heart out of their flesh, and give them a heart of flesh. (NKJV)

**Ezekiel 39:26**

> They will forget their humiliation and all their rebellions against me when they live securely on their fertile land with no one to frighten them. (CEV)

**1 Samuel 12:24**

> The people will forget their shame and how they rejected me when they live again in safety on their own land with no one to make them afraid. (NCV)

**Psalm 111:10**

> The fear of the Lord is the beginning of wisdom; all those who practice it have a good understanding. His praise endures forever. (NRSV)

**Job 42:10**

> And the Lord restored the fortunes of Job, when he had prayed for his friends; and the Lord gave Job twice as much as he had before. (RSV)

**Luke 3:5**

> Every valley will be filled, and every mountain and hill will be leveled. The crooked will be made straight and the rough places made smooth. (CEB)

**Revelation 21:6**

> Everything is finished! I am Alpha and Omega, the beginning and the end. I will freely give water from the life-giving fountain to everyone who is thirsty. (CEV)

**1 John 1:9**

> If we confess our sins, he is faithful and just to forgive us our sins and to cleanse us from all unrighteousness. (ESV)

**Titus 2:1**

That is the way we should live, because God's grace that can save everyone has come. It teaches us not to live against God nor to do the evil things the world wants to do. Instead, that grace teaches us to live in the present age in a wise and right way and in a way that shows we serve God. We should live like that while we wait for our great hope and the coming of the glory of our great God and Savior Jesus Christ. (NCV)

**2 Peter 3:14**

And so, dear friends, while you are waiting for these things to happen, make every effort to be found living peaceful lives that are pure and blameless in his sight. (NLT)

**Revelation 22:17**

And the Spirit and the bride say, "Come!" And let him who hears say, "Come!" And let him who thirsts come. Whoever desires, let him take the water of life freely. (NKJV)

# To the Promise Land We Will Go

We pass through life in stages. It takes time to grow and mature in the way of the Kingdom. We were never meant to perpetually circle or remain in one season of life like the children of Israel, who wandered in the wilderness for forty years for lack of faith. We must move on to the Promise Land. There you will build your home, increase and prosper.

Therefore, there is a new season in life awaiting you.

**Deuteronomy 8:1**

> Be careful to follow every command I am giving you today, so that you may live and increase and may enter and possess the land the LORD promised on oath to your ancestors. (NIV)

# THE WARRIOR

**Summer**

*In Summer's Sun I want to run*
*Run from the heat*
*of the day*
*The battle drags on and on*
*Shelter me, Oh big tree*
*Set me free from the violent ray*
*Relentlessly in the heat of the day*
*Oh that a refreshing spring would rescue me*
*from the sun's enmity*

# Journey to the Promise Land

This is the season of a long, hot summer; a season of striving. The battle drags on and on, relentlessly. These dry, thirsty times, can last for many years. The Promise Land represents abundance and blessings for the Christian, but obedience always precedes the blessings. Blessings are the conditional reward for obedience. Blessings are what the Lord wants to lavish on us. We who have been born again, have life. Loved unconditionally, we have eternal life, but in order to have a more abundant and prosperous life, one must submit to the will of the Lord, obey His commands and learn many lessons in the process. Obedience goes against our natural self - our sinful flesh man. We find that we are at war within ourselves, as well as at war in the heavenly, spiritual sense.

There is abundant fruit in the Promise Land, but there are also battles to fight and wars to wage. God not only desires to save us and take us out of our bondage, but he desires to bring us into the Land of Promise - the land of blessings, as he did with the children of Israel. So often, we are brought by the way of the wilderness, because it is in our bareness that we find true worship.

**Numbers 14:8**

If the Lord is pleased with us, he'll bring us into this land and give it to us. It's a land that's full of milk and honey. (CEB)

**Deuteronomy 5:33**

Stay on the path that the Lord your God has commanded you to follow. Then you will live long and prosperous lives in the land you are about to enter and occupy. (NLT)

**Deuteronomy 10:12**

So now, O Israel, what does the Lord your God require of you? Only to fear the Lord your God, to walk in all his ways, to love him, to serve the Lord your God with all your heart and with all your soul. (NRSV)

**Leviticus 26:13**

I am the LORD your God, who brought you out of Egypt so that you would no longer be slaves to the Egyptians; I broke the bars of your yoke and enabled you to walk with heads held high. (NIV)

**Romans 6:16-17**

Do you not know that if you yield yourselves to any one as obedient slaves, you are slaves of the one whom you obey, either of sin, which leads to death, or of obedience, which leads to righteousness? But thanks be to God, that you who were once slaves of sin have become obedient from the heart to the standard of teaching to which you were committed. (RSV)

# The Wilderness

Obedience requires great personal sacrifice. The cost will require your life itself. No warrior wants to die, but most warriors are willing to die. Obedience to God will require that we lay ourselves upon the sacrificial table and die to self, as Abraham was asked to lay his son upon the sacrificial altar and as God himself required his own son to die for us.

The wilderness experiences are not pleasant, but necessary, to test what is in our own heart so that we are completely assured of the Father's love. If we are ever to be consistent in our obedience and advance in his divine life, we must be convinced of the Father's divine love.

During the testing in these dark valleys, you will hear the Father saying, "Will you trust me?" The enormous pressure of these trials will determine if you will trust Him or if you will escape, taking matters into your own hands.

**Exodus 20:20**

> Moses said to the people, "Don't be afraid, because God has come only to test you and to make sure you are always in awe of God so that you don't sin." (CEB)

**Deuteronomy 8:2**

Remember how the LORD your God led you all the way in the wilderness these forty years, to humble and test you in order to know what was in your heart, whether or not you would keep his commands. (NIV)

**Deuteronomy 8:16**

Don't forget how the Lord your God has led you through the desert for the past forty years. He wanted to find out if you were truly willing to obey him and depend on him. (CEV)

**Isaiah 1:19**

If you willingly obey me, the best crops in the land will be yours. (CEV)

**John 16:33**

I have said these things to you, that in me you may have peace. In the world you will have tribulation. But take heart; I have overcome the world." (ESV)

**Psalm 139:23**

Investigate my life, O God, find out everything about me; Cross-examine and test me, get a clear picture of what I'm about; See for yourself whether I've done anything wrong— then guide me on the road to eternal life. (MSG)

# No Battle is Useless

Although many failed battles have severe consequences, many great lessons are learned in order to take on greater battles in the future. Therefore no battle is useless, for all things will work together for our good. This is a solemn promise, if we love the Lord our God and are called according to his purpose. Since the Father, our Maker, knows what our greatest needs are and that he loves us dearly, we can rest assured that he has our best interest at heart.

**Psalm 42:11**

> Why, my soul, are you downcast? Why so disturbed within me? Put your hope in God, for I will yet praise him, my Savior and my God. (NIV)

**Joshua 1:8**

> This book of the law shall not depart from your mouth, but you shall meditate on it day and night, so that you may be careful to do according to all that is written in it; for then

you will make your way prosperous, and then you will have success. (NASB)

**Luke 6:46**

"Why do you call me, 'Lord, Lord,' but do not do what I say? (NCV)

**Nehemiah 9:17**

They refused to obey, and didn't remember the wonders that you accomplished in their midst. They acted arrogantly and decided to return to their slavery in Egypt. But you are a God ready to forgive, merciful and compassionate, very patient, and truly faithful. You didn't forsake them. (CEB)

**1 Samuel 12:22**

For the sake of His reputation, He will not cast away His chosen people. Before you ever chose Him, the Eternal One chose you as His own because it pleased Him. (VOICE)

**Romans 8:28**

And we know that for those who love God all things work together for good, for those who are called according to his purpose. (ESV)

Summer is the season I learned that you don't win all the battles. Sometimes you learn to just get back up again. This is a painful time as you suffer through many hurts and don't understand what God is doing in your life. You may have seen many of churches split or you may have experienced the death of a child. This is where the rubber meets the road. It is times like these, when you learn to surrender and trust in His goodness. This is what is meant in Ephesians 6:13, to stand your ground and remain firm with all your armor intact. Remain trusting in his righteousness his truth, his just and perfect ways. Keeping our eyes on him and not on others is crucial. For many will disappoint us.

The main thing is to not let your faith be shipwrecked, or stuck in any one season of life, but to experience all of Him - for at the end of the long summer is the harvest.

**1 Timothy 1:19**

> Having faith and a good conscience, which some having rejected, concerning the faith have suffered shipwreck. (NKJV)

**Psalm 78:9-11**

> The men of Ephraim, though armed with bows, turned back on the day of battle; they did not keep God's covenant and refused to live by his law. They forgot what he had done, the wonders he had shown them. (NIV)

**Galatians 3:3-5**

> How foolish can you be? After starting your Christian lives in the Spirit, why are you now trying to become perfect by your own human effort? Have you experienced so much for nothing? Surely it was not in vain, was it? I ask you again, does God give you the Holy Spirit and work miracles among you because you obey the law? Of course not! It is because you believe the message you heard about Christ. (NLT)

**Philippians 1:27**

Only, live your life in a manner worthy of the gospel of Christ, so that, whether I come and see you or am absent and hear about you, I will know that you are standing firm in one spirit, striving side by side with one mind for the faith of the gospel. (NRSV)

**Philippians 3:7-9**

But whatever gain I had, I counted as loss for the sake of Christ. Indeed I count everything as loss because of the surpassing worth of knowing Christ Jesus my Lord. For his sake I have suffered the loss of all things, and count them as refuse, in order that I may gain Christ and be found in him, not having a righteousness of my own, based on law, but that which is through faith in Christ, the righteousness from God that depends on faith. (RSV)

**2 Timothy 1:12**

For this reason I also suffer these things; nevertheless I am not ashamed, for I know whom I have believed and am persuaded that He is able to keep what I have committed to Him until that Day. (NKJV)

# *Trials and Tests*

During this season in my life, I remember the time I prayed for an older man in a wheelchair, for his healing. If ever there were a time in my life I felt strong in my faith it was at this time. I had studied every scripture on faith in my concordance. It seemed to me that my faith was strong. I prayed for God to deliver this man from his crippled state. I shouted out every scripture I knew in very warlike shouts proclaiming this man's healing. Yet, nothing happened. I than took a cup of water and poured it on his head for no apparent reason, other than desperately wanting to see God do something. Never had I mustered so much faith before in all my life, but it seemed, nothing happened. I could not understand why God would not heal this crippled man. At this same time, I had a friend die of cancer. This is the dead of summer.

For a time I doubted without understanding. I did not doubt that God could heal or, that he was God, but I wanted to know why I could not operate in the power of Christ, in healing and signs and wonders, as I believe, every young Christian wants to do. I wanted to save the world, have great favor and influence many people's lives. I longed to see the possibilities of actual heaven on earth. I didn't realize it was I, the Lord wanted to change, first.

Later after much asking, wrestling and contemplating, did I learn that God had a sovereign will that I could not impose on. Perhaps, God did do something internal in this man's life. I don't know for certain. But for some reason, God did not see fit to answer my prayer as I thought he should. This is the sovereign way of God. His ways are higher than our ways. Possibly, he knew that my pride would become a serious problem that would later lead to my downfall. Even though I was learning to use the authority of God's Word, there was so much to learn about his timing, fasting and the gift of healing, itself. Later I would learn that we cannot move ahead of God, rather, we move with God. God must lead and we must follow.

In addition to this new insight, I also had to admit I didn't really know all there was to know. There was still yet more to learn. In humility, I would return to the schoolmaster time and time again.

**Psalm 81:7**

> You cried out to Me, I heard your distress, and I delivered you; I answered you from the secret place, where clouds of thunder roll. I tested you at the waters of Meribah. (VOICE)

**Hosea 4:6**

> My people are destroyed for lack of knowledge: because thou hast rejected knowledge. . . (KJV)

**2 Samuel 7:28**

> And now, O Lord God, You are God, and Your words are truth, and You have promised this good thing to Your servant. (AMP)

**2 Chronicles 26:16**

But after Uzziah became powerful, his pride led to his downfall. He was unfaithful to the LORD his God, and entered the temple of the LORD to burn incense on the altar of incense. (NIV)

**Isaiah 55:9**

Just as the heavens are higher than the earth, so are my ways higher than your ways, and my plans than your plans. (CEB)

**Romans 12:6**

God has also given each of us different gifts to use. If we can prophesy, we should do it according to the amount of faith we have. (CEV)

# Wounded in Battle

This is what summer is like, doing everything you think you know is right but, having to accept that you just don't know all that you think you know and there is still more yet to learn. This may be a time when people lose faith in the God they thought they knew and served and give up the faith.

In Matthew 13, Jesus speaks of the farmer who sowed and some seed fell upon the rocks and the seed sprang up a sprout but, when the sun came up, the plant was scorched because it had no root. The person who received the word with joy did not withstand the time of trouble or persecution because the root was shallow. Other seed fell among thorns, which grew up and choked the plants. This person allowed the worries of this life and deceitfulness of wealth to choke it and render it unfruitful.

**Jeremiah 50:6**

> My people have been like lost sheep. Their shepherds led them the wrong way and caused them to wander away into the mountains and hills. They forgot where their resting place was. (ERV)

**Hosea 13:5-6**

I took care of you in the wilderness, in that dry and thirsty land. But when you had eaten and were satisfied, you became proud and forgot me. (NLT)

**Isaiah 40:31**

Why would you ever complain, O Jacob, or, whine, Israel, saying, "God has lost track of me. He doesn't care what happens to me"? Don't you know anything? Haven't you been listening? God doesn't come and go. God lasts. He's Creator of all you can see or imagine. He doesn't get tired out, doesn't pause to catch his breath. And he knows everything, inside and out. He energizes those who get tired, gives fresh strength to dropouts. For even young people tire and drop out, young folk in their prime stumble and fall. But those who wait upon God get fresh strength. They spread their wings and soar like eagles,They run and don't get tired, they walk and don't lag behind. (MSG)

**Isaiah 57:10**

"You were tired out by the length of your road, Yet you did not say, 'It is hopeless.' You found renewed strength,Therefore you did not faint. (NASB)

**Matthew 13:20-22**

And what is the seed that fell on rocky ground? That seed is like the person who hears the teaching and quickly accepts it with joy. But he does not let the teaching go deep into his life, so he keeps it only a short time. When trouble or persecution comes because of the teaching he accepted, he quickly gives up. And what is the seed that fell among the thorny weeds? That seed is like the person who hears the teaching but lets worries about this life and the temptation of wealth stop that teaching from growing. So the teaching does not produce fruit in that person's life. (NCV)

**1 Peter 2:20-21**

But if you suffer for doing good and you endure it, this is commendable before God. To this you were called, because Christ suffered for you, leaving you an example, that you should follow in his steps. (NIV)

**Romans 9:22-23**

Who in the world do you think you are to second-guess God? Do you for one moment suppose any of us knows enough to call God into question? Clay doesn't talk back to the fingers that mold it, saying, "Why did you shape me like this?" Isn't it obvious that a potter has a perfect right to shape one lump of clay into a vase for holding flowers and another into a pot for cooking beans? If God needs one style of pottery especially designed to show his angry displeasure and another style carefully crafted to show his glorious goodness, isn't that all right? (MGS)

# Wrestling through Prayer

The Lord has answered many of my prayers, like when my daughter had pneumonia, heart failure and heart surgery all before she was nearly five months old. When her condition was fragile and she was struggling for life, the Lord brought her through this difficult time with much success. The Lord has, indeed, answered many of my prayers immediately.

Other answered prayers, were the many times each day, I prayed for my car to start in the morning, when my starter sounded as though it would barely turn over. Many days in my hurry to rush my children off to school, as a single-mom, and get off to work, the Lord would faithfully start my old run-down car.

Another time, I prayed for an angel to sit on my hood as I ascended the steep hill to drive to work, on this particular dangerous pass. My hood did not seem to shut just right and if it were to fly open while I traveled to work, I would likely have been in a very serious car accident. I asked the Lord, specifically, if he would protect me and allow an angel to sit on my hood. I believe an angel sat on my hood and protected me the many days I drove this pass.

But one very hot summer day, while I was driving home another way, my car hood did fly up and shattered my windshield. I was able to safely pull on to the shoulder. There have been so many times the Lord has been so good to hear my plea for help and answer my many prayers accordingly. There are too many to record.

Yet it seems even though God has worked mightily in response to my prayers, there are times that the Lord will have me wrestle with him for a long period of time before answering my prayers. Like Jacob, the Lord wants me to undergo change. The Lord loves us too much to allow us to stay in our vessels of flesh. There must be a circumcision of the heart - a cutting away of the fleshy heart to signify the covenant of salvation. By covenant we must forsake all other gods to give God first place in our hearts.

**Hebrews 1:14**

> Of course, you get no credit for being patient if you are beaten for doing wrong. But if you suffer for doing good and endure it patiently, God is pleased with you. For God called you to do good, even if it means suffering, just as Christ suffered for you. He is your example, and you must follow in his steps. (NLT)

**Psalm 6:9**

> The Lord has heard my request for mercy. The Lord has accepted my prayer. (ERV)

**Nehemiah 1:6**

> Let your ear be attentive and your eyes open to hear the prayer of your servant that I now pray before you day and night for your servants, the people of Israel, confessing the sins of the people of Israel, which we have sinned against you. Both I and my family have sinned. (NRSV)

**1 Chronicles 5:20**

And they were helped against them, and the Hagarites were delivered into their hand, and all that were with them: for they cried to God in the battle, and he was intreated of them; because they put their trust in him. (KJV)

**Colossians 2:11**

In him you were also circumcised with the circumcision made without hands, by putting off the body of the sins of the flesh, by the circumcision of Christ. (NKJV)

**2 Corinthians 3:18**

And we all, who with unveiled faces contemplate the Lord's glory, are being transformed into his image with ever-increasing glory, which comes from the Lord, who is the Spirit. (NIV)

# Humility

Jacob was on his way home. Home is typically the place we call rest, but for Jacob home is where the shadows were left behind in the closet, like we so often have done. "I want you to deal with it now," God seemed to be saying. Esau, Jacobs twin brother, had intent to kill Jacob when he had left his hometown years ago, now Jacob would have to face Esau in the land of Seir, the country of Edom. Jacob sends a message ahead that he comes in peace but the message returned is that Esau is also coming to meet Jacob with four hundred men. This is not a good sign that all is well and forgiven. Jacob prayed with humility and reminded God how God had said to him "Go back to your country and your relatives, and I will make you prosper." Here is where Jacob wrestles with the spoken word of God versus the unlikely circumstances.

I love that God allowed himself to be so earthly in order to touch and heal us. Imagine wrestling with God. His hands all over you, pressing against you. This pressure is what transforms us. You can trust that pressure in the Potter's hands is going to create a marvelous miracle.

**Genesis 32:9**

Jacob said, "Lord, God of my father Abraham, God of my father Isaac, who said to me, 'Go back to your country and your relatives, and I'll make sure things go well for you,' (CEB)

**Psalm 13:2**

How long must I wrestle with my thoughts and day after day have sorrow in my heart? How long will my enemy triumph over me? (NIV)

**Genesis 32:11**

Please rescue me from my brother. I am afraid he will come and attack not only me, but my wives and children as well. (CEV)

**2 Kings 22:19**

Because your heart was responsive and you humbled yourself before the LORD when you heard what I have spoken against this place and its people—that they would become a curse and be laid waste—and because you tore your robes and wept in my presence, I also have heard you, declares the LORD. (NIV)

**2 Chronicles 7:14**

If my people, which are called by my name, shall humble themselves, and pray, and seek my face, and turn from their wicked ways; then will I hear from heaven, and will forgive their sin, and will heal their land. (KJV)

**Genesis 32:12**

For You said, 'I will surely prosper you and make your descendants as the sand of the sea, which is too great to be numbered.'" (NASB)

# Jacob Struggles with God

Jacob first tries in his own flesh to resolve the problem by his own method. He sets up a plan to manipulate his brother, to soften him with gifts of wealth. That night, as Jacob sent his servants ahead to meet with Esau, Jacob took his family and all his possessions and sent them across the stream. Jacob was alone and there he spent time with God. Jacob wrestled with a man - not recognizing it was God (Gen. 32:28). They wrestled till daybreak and Jacob would not give up. So, the God-man, who is Jesus himself, touched the socket of Jacob's hip - the strongest tendon of the body and still Jacob would not give up. Jacob asked the man to bless him and the God-man changed Jacob's name to Israel.

At some point, Jacob must have realized that he was not just fighting an ordinary battle of flesh and blood, but a spiritual battle and that he needed to persevere with everything that he had within him. As we wrestle with God he will touch our strongest area of resistance in order to show us our idolatry, with a desire to strengthen us in our weaknesses. God had to break Jacob and yet Jacob held out and said, "Bless me." God did indeed bless Jacob. But God also changed Jacob and he was never the same again. He changed his name and the way he walked. God desires to transform us too. He desires to change our old habits and replace them with newness of life, until we are conformed to the likeness of his Son. For we were created to be in his image.

**Genesis 32:28**

> Then the man said, "Your name will no longer be Jacob. Your name will now be Israel, because you have wrestled with God and with people, and you have won." (NCV)

**Psalm 68:20**

> Our God is a God Who sets us free. The way out of death belongs to God the Lord. (NLV)

**Luke 5:38**

> New wine must be stored in new wineskins. (NLT)

**Isaiah 43:19**

> I am about to do a new thing; now it springs forth, do you not perceive it? I will make a way in the wilderness and rivers in the desert. (NRSV)

**Romans 8:29**

> For those God foreknew he also predestined to be conformed to the image of his Son, that he might be the firstborn among many brothers and sisters. (NIV)

**Isaiah 41:10**

> So don't be afraid. I am here, with you; don't be dismayed, for I am your God. I will strengthen you, help you. I am

here with My right hand to make right and to hold you up. (VOICE)

**Psalm 18:32-35**

It is God who arms me with strength, and makes my way perfect. He makes my feet like the feet of deer, and sets me on my high places. He teaches my hands to make war, so that my arms can bend a bow of bronze. You have also given me the shield of Your salvation; your right hand has held me up, your gentleness has made me great. (NKJV)

**Isaiah 62:2**

Nations will see your righteousness, all kings your glory. You will be called by a new name, which the Lord's own mouth will determine. (CEB)

**Revelation 2:17**

If you have ears, listen to what the Spirit says to the churches. To everyone who wins the victory, I will give some of the hidden food. I will also give each one a white stone with a new name written on it. No one will know that name except the one who is given the stone. (CEV)

# Identity in Christ

The Bride must never forget her identity is in Jesus Christ, otherwise fear and hopelessness will set in. When we look at the problems in the world and the problems with our government, our church, crime and corruption and our problems in our own homes and forget to look at who is the answer, or how big our God is, it is easy to slip into depression. If Satan can get us to feel helpless, less worth, less value, less talented and less intelligent, we would begin to feel defeated. If defeated, we will lose hope and remain empty, dry and lifeless.

**1 John 4:4**

> Little children, you are from God and have overcome them, for he who is in you is greater than he who is in the world. (ESV)

**2 Corinthians 5:21**

> For He made Him who knew no sin to be sin for us, that we might become the righteousness of God in Him. (NKJV)

**1 Thessalonians 5:5**

> You belong to the light and live in the day. We don't live in the night or belong to the dark. (CEV)

**Romans 8:17**

> If we are God's children, we will get the blessings God has for his people. He will give us all that he has given Christ. But we must suffer like Christ suffered. Then we will be able to share his glory. (ERV)

**Deuteronomy 28:13**

> The LORD will make you the head, not the tail. If you pay attention to the commands of the LORD your God that I give you this day and carefully follow them, you will always be at the top, never at the bottom. (NIV)

**1 Peter 2:9**

> But you are a chosen people, royal priests, a holy nation, a people for God's own possession. You were chosen to tell about the wonderful acts of God, who called you out of darkness into his wonderful light. (NCV)

I remember a time when I was young, I struggled in school. My family moved often and I was bounced from one school to another. This one particular day, I was in school and I was having a difficult time. I was about nine years old and I was taken to the principal, when he determined that I should go home. It seems, I was was unable to keep it together. I was normally not a disruptive child or misbehaved, but I was listening to a familiar voice in my head that told me I was a failure, and that I was not smart, and I would never amount to anything. This is the same thing Satan tells me today. Many times while entertaining these thoughts, I struggle to believe in myself. When I am not confident in myself I tend to imagine others are not confident in me. I feel estranged and incomplete. Whenever I feel that I am being treated poorly, it seems as though, the lies in my head seem to confirm and agree with all the previous experiences of failure and rejection in my life. An immobilizing feeling of depression comes over me, a feeling I have battled many times over. Trying to decide if anyone feels I have any value or worth and sadly, even questioning God's love for me.

Often I've fallen into a trap of comparing my life with someone else's life. Given into self-righteousness and pride, I'll state my case to God about how I am more faithful and walk so much more upright than another person and yet their life may seem to have all the elements of spiritual and relational bliss. If we are comparing our lives to others to see if God loves us we are going to fall under a big trap of dissatisfaction. God loves us all the same. He died for us all. Why would a Christian feel so unloved and so unworthy? Because she has forgotten her true identity.

When Caleb and Joshua of the Bible, surveyed the land the Lord had promised them, they encouraged the Israelites that they were well able to possess the land, in spite of the fact the people in this land looked liked giants. God's people looked liked grasshoppers by comparison (Joshua 14). Because of Israel's low self-image and self-belittling of themselves they could not bring themselves to dream the bold dream God was giving them and that was to go and possess the land of milk and honey - the Promise Land. God's people could not even envision it. Even though, we are his own body, we too find it hard to believe that we are able to do the impossible. This is why we are told in 1 Corinthians 2:16 to put on the mind of Christ. We are in fact the temple of the Holy Spirit. The Holy Spirit uses our physical bodies and minds to carry out the Lord's will upon the earth. We are Christ ambassadors sent into the world to do the work of the Father.

**1 Corinthians 6:19-20**

You should know that your body is a temple for the Holy Spirit that you received from God and that lives in you. You don't own yourselves. God paid a very high price to make you his. So honor God with your body. (ERV)

**Acts 17:28**

'In him we live and move and have our being'; as even some of your own poets have said, "'For we are indeed his offspring.' (ESV)

**Mark 16:15**

And He said to them, "Go into all the world and preach the gospel to all creation. (NASB)

**Philippians 2:13**

Because God is working in you to help you want to do and be able to do what pleases him. (NCV)

**Matthew 19:26**

But Jesus looked at them and said, "With man this is impossible, but with God all things are possible." (ESV)

There are women today desperately crying out to find meaning and hope in their lives. Our dreams our destroyed by discontentment and self-condemnation. We find it difficult to see our full potential as a daughter of God because we are filled with fear, doubt, inferiority and inadequacy. Yet, God created the universe from nothing; surely we can believe he can make something beautiful out of our lives. When we choose to focus on our own perspectives we ignore God's awesome omniscient power to believe in our own minuscule view of life. When we have a God-perspective we see that God is still in control. Our quest is not to understand all of this life but to believe that the one who created and designed this life has a purpose in each of our lives.

**Philippians 3:20-21**

> For our citizenship is in heaven, from which we also eagerly wait for the Savior, the Lord Jesus Christ, who will transform our lowly body that it may be conformed to His glorious body, according to the working by which He is able even to subdue all things to Himself. (NKJV)

**2 Timothy 2:25-26**

> Be gentle when you try to teach those who are against what you say. God may change their hearts so they will turn to the truth. Then they will know they had been held in a trap by the devil to do what he wanted them to do. But now they are able to get out of it. (NLV)

**Romans 8:15**

> For you did not receive a spirit of slavery to fall back into fear, but you have received a spirit of adoption. When we cry, "Abba! Father!" (NRSV)

**Philippians 1:6**

> Being confident of this very thing, that he which hath begun a good work in you will perform it until the day of Jesus Christ: (KJV)

**1 John 4:4**

Children, you belong to God, and you have defeated these enemies. God's Spirit is in you and is more powerful than the one that is in the world. (CEV)

**Proverbs 19:21**

Many are the plans in a person's heart, but it is the LORD's purpose that prevails. (NIV)

**Jeremiah 29:11**

I say this because I know the plans that I have for you." This message is from the Lord. "I have good plans for you. I don't plan to hurt you. I plan to give you hope and a good future. (ERV)

**John 16:33**

I have said these things to you, that in me you may have peace. In the world you will have tribulation. But take heart; I have overcome the world." (ESV)

# World of Wars

The Warrior realizes from past experience that she must protect her investment in the Kingdom by fighting the good fight of faith. She must not put her guard down because her enemy comes to steal, kill and destroy and the enemy never sleeps. The Lord, *her husband*, has entrusted her with many valuable possessions and she has learned of a valuable weapon of warfare - prayer. The words of the Lord are powerful to pull down the strongholds of his enemies (2 Cor. 10:4). By speaking forth the powerful Word of the Lord and his praises, the enemy is disarmed.

The *Bride* learns to know the voice of God through an intimate love relationship that he has initiated. The *Warrior* learns to know the voice of God through her knowledge of the scriptures. It is through declaring God's Word that she defeats her enemies, as in the example that Jesus gave when he defeated Satan in the wilderness (Matt. 4).

Jesus was faithful and demonstrated his qualification to become the Savior of all who receive him. Because Jesus was tempted in every way just as we are, he became our merciful and faithful high priest. When tempted in the wilderness, Jesus did not yield to Satan by using his supernatural power for his own needs. Jesus did not use his power to win a large following by miracles or magic. Jesus did not compromise with Satan or take shortcuts, as we so often do. How did Jesus defeat Satan? Jesus defeated Satan by using a weapon that we too have at our disposal, the sword of the Spirit, which is the word of God (Eph. 6:17). In the gospel of John, Jesus says, he is the Word. It is the spoken word in the authority of the name Jesus, that Satan must back down, turn and run. However we must declare it and believe it, without doubting.

But merely speaking God's word is only part of the answer, we must also have forgiveness in our hearts toward our brothers and sisters. For without forgiveness in our hearts our prayers are hindered.

**John 1:14**

> And the Word became flesh, and dwelt among us, and we saw His glory, glory as of the only begotten from the Father, full of grace and truth. (NASB)

**1 Thessalonians 2:13**

> Also, we always thank God because when you heard his message from us, you accepted it as the word of God, not the words of humans. And it really is God's message which works in you who believe. (NCV)

**Isaiah 55:11**

> So shall my word be that goes out from my mouth; it shall not return to me empty, but it shall accomplish that which I purpose, and shall succeed in the thing for which I sent it. (ESV)

## John 10:10

The thief does not come except to steal, and to kill, and to destroy. I have come that they may have life, and that they may have it more abundantly. (NKJV)

## James 5:16-17

Therefore, confess your sins to one another, and pray for one another so that you may be healed. The effective prayer of a righteous man can accomplish much. (NASB)

## Colossians 2:15

In this way, he disarmed the spiritual rulers and authorities. He shamed them publicly by his victory over them on the cross. (NLT)

## Ephesians 6:17-18

Take the helmet of salvation, and the sword of the Spirit, which is the word of God. Pray in the Spirit at all times in every prayer and supplication. To that end keep alert and always persevere in supplication for all the saints. (NRSV)

## James 1:22-24

But be doers of the word, and not hearers only, deceiving yourselves. For if any one is a hearer of the word and not a doer, he is like a man who observes his natural face in a mirror; for he observes himself and goes away and at once forgets what he was like. (RSV)

# The Battles

The violence of war wages on. The enemy seems to plunder and we are like loot to him. But do not be afraid, even if you walk through the shadow of death, the one who knows our name, who created and formed us in the womb will redeem us. He will see us to the end and set our feet on firm ground.

There are different wars to be fought. There is war in the heavenly places. There is war against our flesh and there is war to advance. All battles require faith. As we fight many battles we are more keenly aware of the forces that seem greater than ourselves. Even still, we are not to focus on how small we are but to focus on how great is our God.

The Lord may ask us to advance to enlarge our territory. Fear is our enemy and once immobilized we will be tricked into believing we are useless for the Kingdom. We cannot become greater yet, until we have learned to conquer fear. We beat our bodies into subjection; we strive for mastery and discipline, but only to receive an incorruptible reward. We discipline ourselves by beating down the flesh, so that we give reign to the spirit within us. We build spiritual muscles, so that *weaklings* become *warriors*.

Yet, we cannot take down enemies or pursue territories in of ourselves. It is not by our own might or by our own power but by his

Spirit that the enemies of Christ are defeated (Zechariah 4:6). The Lord is raising up an army of people that will go out and do the will of the Father just as he has shown us.

Although the Lord fights our battles, our job is to confess our sins before Him and listen to do his will, to obey and follow him. For grace is free, but the Kingdom will cost you everything!

**Psalm 32:4-5**

> Day and night, Your hand kept pressing on me. My strength dried up like water in the summer heat; You wore me down. When I finally saw my own lies, I owned up to my sins before You, and I did not try to hide my evil deeds from You. I said to myself, "I'll admit all my sins to the Eternal," and You lifted and carried away the guilt of my sin. (VOICE)

**Ephesians 6:12**

> For we wrestle not against flesh and blood, but against principalities, against powers, against the rulers of the darkness of this world, against spiritual wickedness in high places. (KJV)

**1 Corinthians 9:27**

> But I discipline my body and bring it into subjection, lest, when I have preached to others, I myself should become disqualified. (NKJV)

**Psalm 144:1**

> Bless the Lord, my rock, who taught my hands how to fight, who taught my fingers how to do battle! (CEB)

**Isaiah 54:15-17**

Behold, they may gather together and stir up strife, but it is not from Me. Whoever stirs up strife against you shall fall and surrender to you. Behold, I have created the smith who blows on the fire of coals and who produces a weapon for its purpose; and I have created the devastator to destroy. But no weapon that is formed against you shall prosper, and every tongue that shall rise against you in judgment you shall show to be in the wrong. This [peace, righteousness, security, triumph over opposition] is the heritage of the servants of the Lord [those in whom the ideal Servant of the Lord is reproduced]; this is the righteousness or the vindication which they obtain from Me [this is that which I impart to them as their justification], says the Lord. (AMP)

**2 Chronicles 20:17**

You don't need to fight this battle. Just take your places, stand ready, and watch how the Lord, who is with you, will deliver you, Judah and Jerusalem. Don't be afraid or discouraged! Go out tomorrow and face them. The Lord will be with you." (CEB)

**Nehemiah 1:6**

Let your ear be attentive and your eyes open, to hear the prayer of your servant that I now pray before you day and night for the people of Israel your servants, confessing the sins of the people of Israel, which we have sinned against you. Even I and my father's house have sinned. (ESV)

**Psalm 51:10**

Create in me a clean heart, O God, and renew a steadfast spirit within me. (NKJV)

**Psalm 51:17**

The sacrifice you desire is a broken spirit. You will not reject a broken and repentant heart, O God. (NLT)

# Faith Walking

Wise people realize they are weak but He is strong. Jesus wants us to understand our authority is entirely through him. Jesus said to his disciples, "Why are you so afraid."

Authority had to be given to the disciples, without the authority of Jesus Christ demons would pay us no attention, but when Jesus Christ name is spoken, every demon must take notice. Let us put on Christ and walk in the protection of his armor, by walking in him and in all his ways.

Eventually, we understand that the battle does not belong to us and it is his alone to fight. The only battle we truly fight ourselves is the fight of faith. We must not lose faith, which ultimately affects our hope and love. Hope is so incredible and unusual it affects our health, finances, marriage, inventions and even our creativity.

**2 Chronicles 20:15**

> "Pay attention, all of Judah, every inhabitant of Jerusalem, and King Jehoshaphat," Jahaziel said. "This is what the Lord says to you: Don't be afraid or discouraged by this great army because the battle isn't yours. It belongs to God! (CEB)

**Psalm 91:14**

The Lord says, "If you love me and truly know who I am, I will rescue you and keep you safe. (CEV)

**2 Samuel 22:18-20**

He saved me from my powerful enemies, who hated me. They were too strong for me, so he saved me. They attacked me in my time of trouble, but the Lord was there to support me. He was pleased with me, so he rescued me. He took me to a safe place. (ERV)

**2 Samuel 22:30, 33-36**

With your help I can advance against a troop; with my God I can scale a wall. It is God who arms me with strength and keeps my way secure. He makes my feet like the feet of a deer; he causes me to stand on the heights. He trains my hands for battle; my arms can bend a bow of bronze. (NIV)

# Hindered Prayers

In of ourselves we lack courage, yet God wants us to be bold as lions and move forward in our lives without any fear. God did not intend for us to be fearful.

In the garden of Eden, where life itself began, there was no fear, because God did not give us a spirit of fear. The spirit of fear came from the father of lies after the *fall*, yet he the father of lies is not your father. Whoever puts his trust in the Lord shall be safe, but whoever lacks faith, their prayers will be hindered. Jesus has told us in scriptures, if we have faith we could heal the sick and that we have power and authority to ask and God will answer us. This will require a complete dependence on Jesus.

But one thing we often forget he warns us, we must forgive anyone whom we have something against. The Bible teaches us that if we are holding anything against our brother God will not hear our prayers. We must first go and make it right with our brother for God to hear our pleas.

Therefore, fear and unforgiveness hinder our prayers and keep us from advancing and growing in the Kingdom of God. When our prayers our hindered we need to apply the blood of Christ by acknowledgement of our sins and repentance. Only the blood of Jesus can wash away our sins and remove them for all eternity. By simply asking for forgiveness of our sins, he is faithful and just to forgive us.

**2 Timothy 1:7**

> For God gave us a spirit not of fear but of power and love and self-control. (ESV)

**John 10:27**

> My sheep hear my voice, and I know them, and they follow me. (KJV)

**Proverbs 28:9**

> When people do not listen to God's teachings, he does not listen to their prayers. (ERV)

**James 1:6-8**

> But let him ask in faith, with no doubting, for the one who doubts is like a wave of the sea that is driven and tossed by the wind. For that person must not suppose that he will receive anything from the Lord; he is a double-minded man, unstable in all his ways. (ESV)

**Psalm 66:18-20**

> If I had cherished sin in my heart, the Lord would not have listened; but God has surely listened and has heard my prayer. Praise be to God, who has not rejected my prayer or withheld his love from me! (NIV)

**Psalm 32:3**

When I refused to confess my sin, my body wasted away, and I groaned all day long. (NLT)

**Mark 11:25**

Whenever you stand praying, forgive, if you have anything against anyone, so that your Father who is in heaven will also forgive you your transgressions. (NASB)

**Matthew 5:23-24**

"So when you offer your gift to God at the altar, and you remember that your brother or sister has something against you, leave your gift there at the altar. Go and make peace with that person, and then come and offer your gift. (NCV)

**Matthew 6:15**

But if you refuse to forgive others, your Father will not forgive your sins. (NLT)

**Luke 6:37**

"Judge not, and you shall not be judged. Condemn not, and you shall not be condemned. Forgive, and you will be forgiven. (NKJV)

**Matthew 7:2**

For with what judgment ye judge, ye shall be judged: and with what measure ye mete, it shall be measured to you again. (KJV)

How long we shall suffer in this season, depends on how long it will take us to go from unbelief to fully trusting and obeying. The Lord told his disciples that he could not do many miracles in his own land because of their unbelief. The principal of believing is very powerful, for even salvation is based upon believing.

**Psalm 78:22**

> For they did not believe in God or trust in his deliverance. (NIV)

**Isaiah 53:1**

> Who has believed our message? To whom has the Lord revealed his powerful arm? (NLT)

**Matthew 21:22**

> Whatever you ask for in prayer with faith, you will receive." (NRSV)

**Matthew 21:32**

> For John came to you in the way of righteousness, and you did not believe him, but the tax collectors and the harlots believed him; and even when you saw it, you did not afterward repent and believe him. (RSV)

**Mark 1:15**

> It's time! The kingdom of God is near! Seek forgiveness, change your actions, and believe this good news! (VOICE)

**Mark 9:23**

Jesus said to him, "If you can believe, all things are possible to him who believes." (NKJV)

**John 5:24**

I assure you, most solemnly I tell you, the person whose ears are open to My words [who listens to My message] and believes and trusts in and clings to and relies on Him Who sent Me has (possesses now) eternal life. And he does not come into judgment [does not incur sentence of judgment, will not come under condemnation], but he has already passed over out of death into life. (AMP)

# Holy Spirit

In this popular movie, Rocky, of the 80's, Rocky Balboa is a small-town, low-wage, boxer. His opponent is a heavy-weight champion. Rocky studied his opponent in order to contemplate his every move. Likewise, Satan and Jesus are enemies. In this corner, Satan - The Destroyer, verses Jesus, in this corner - The Redeemer. The Holy Spirit is our personal trainer. The work of the Holy Spirit is to bring glory to the Savior and reveal to us the spiritual truths that we so often struggle with. The Spirit of truth will guide us in this journey of life and will teach us our father's heart and desires. The Holy Spirit will show you how to pray and what things you need to ask for. Without the help of the Holy Spirit we often pray and ask for things that are not of the will of the Father.

When Jesus ascended back to the throne he gave us the indwelling of the Holy Spirit. It is this anointing that allows us to become like him.

**John 16:13-14**

> However, when the Spirit of Truth comes, he will guide you
> in all truth. He won't speak on his own, but will say whatever
> he hears and will proclaim to you what is to come. He will

glorify me, because he will take what is mine and proclaim it to you. (CEB)

**John 16:12-15**

"I still have many things to tell you, but you can't handle them now. But when the Friend comes, the Spirit of the Truth, he will take you by the hand and guide you into all the truth there is. He won't draw attention to himself, but will make sense out of what is about to happen and, indeed, out of all that I have done and said. He will honor me; he will take from me and deliver it to you. Everything the Father has is also mine. That is why I've said, 'He takes from me and delivers to you.' (The Message, MSG)

**Romans 8:27**

God already knows our deepest thoughts. And he understands what the Spirit is saying, because the Spirit speaks for his people in the way that agrees with what God wants. (ERV)

**James 4:3**

You ask and do not receive, because you ask with wrong motives, so that you may spend it on your pleasures. (NASB)

# Three Enemies

Like Rocky, in this fictional boxing movie we need to study our enemy, in order to be aware of his tactics and schemes. Let us take a closer look at three of the enemies of Christ Jesus: Satan, the World and our Flesh. Satan is the subtle instigator and archenemy of God, whose desire it is to destroy our lives and the lives of our loved ones and causes us to doubt God's Word. Satan's goal has always been to alienate man from God. He is the father of lies and only uses half-truths, if he tells any truth at all. Lies lead to mistrust and broken relationships. Satan merely needs but a foot in the door to do so much damage. Satan uses lies to steal your self-esteem and dignity, as well as, any other thing of worth in your life.

Satan's aim is to go for the kill, but if God does not will it, he will surely try to wear you down and immobilize you. Depression sets in when we find that our actions do not make a difference or impact on what happens to us or in the lives of the people we love. Though we try to make a difference in this world, we begin to take on the mindset of failure. Passivity, lack of assertiveness and indecisiveness placates our thought process, until we our wounded and warped.

**1 Peter 5:8**

Stay alert! Watch out for your great enemy, the devil. He prowls around like a roaring lion, looking for someone to devour. (NLT)

**Proverbs 3:13**

Happy is the man who finds wisdom, and the man who gains understanding, (NKJV)

**1 Corinthians 15:34**

Come back to your senses as you ought, and stop sinning; for there are some who are ignorant of God - I say this to your shame. (NIV)

# Satan

Twenty-Seven, years ago, Satan tried to deceive me into aborting my daughter. I went into a planned parent clinic for a free pregnancy test. When I found that I was positively with child, I was counseled to abort my child, due to the fact, that I was a young, unwed, nineteen year old girl. All logical arguments would have agreed to such a solution; in fact, I had not truly been in love with her father. I had gotten myself in this predicament. This was my second child. I knew that if I gave birth to this child, I would lose any chance of reconciling with my firstborn child's father. Since we were very young, my son's father had promised he would marry me later. All my dreams of a future lie with the father of my firstborn.

Consequently, this decision of abortion weighed heavily on my mind. Based on my knowledge of God's Word, I knew it was wrong to abort my child. I knew God had created her. I also knew that he had allowed me to follow my own desires, to go my own way for a time, blinded by Satan - the god of this age. I knew that my sin had found me out and I could hide no longer. God wanted me to come out clean and he would use my daughter to bring me back to my senses. My daughter was not aborted. Gena was born with Down Syndrome - a type of retardation.

In spite of this condition, Gena remains one of my biggest blessings. I will never regret that I made the right choice at a particularly desperate time in my life. I learned over time that people make desperate choices when they are in desperate situations and they won't always make the right choices during these times. A ply of Satan is to get you and I in desperate circumstances. Desperation most often breeds victims. Satan wants nothing more than for us to curse God and give up. I learned that every desperate choice that we make, is life changing, therefore we cannot afford to be deceived. The only way to expose Satan's lies are to know the word of God and remain close to the Lord. Satan is looking for every opportunity to destroy our lives and immobilize us.

**Ephesians 4:27**

Do not give the devil a foothold. (NIV)

**Matthew 12:29**

For who is powerful enough to enter the house of a strong man like Satan and plunder his goods? Only someone even stronger—someone who could tie him up and then plunder his house. (NLT)

**Job 2:9**

Job's wife said to him, "Are you still clinging to your integrity? Curse God, and die." (CEB)

**John 8:43-45**

Why do you misunderstand what I say? It is because you are unable to hear what I am saying. [You cannot bear to listen to My message; your ears are shut to My teaching.] You are of your father, the devil, and it is your will to practice the lusts and gratify the desires [which are characteristic] of your father. He was a murderer from the beginning and does not stand in the truth, because there is no truth in him. When he speaks a falsehood, he speaks what is natural to him, for he is a liar [himself] and the father of lies and of all that is false. But because I speak the truth, you do not believe Me [do not trust Me, do not rely on Me, or adhere to Me]. (AMP)

**Matthew 13:19**

Whenever people hear the word about the kingdom and don't understand it, the evil one comes and carries off what was planted in their hearts. This is the seed that was sown on the path. (CEB)

**Jeremiah 18:12**

But I know you won't listen. You might as well answer, "We don't care what you say. We have made plans to sin, and we are going to be stubborn and do what we want!" (CEV)

**Proverbs 10:9**

Whoever walks in integrity walks securely, but he who makes his ways crooked will be found out. (ESV)

**Jeremiah 29:11**

I say this because I know the plans that I have for you." This message is from the Lord. "I have good plans for you. I don't plan to hurt you. I plan to give you hope and a good future. (ERV)

# Satan – God's Archenemy

We should know that first, Satan - God's archenemy, wants everything that God wants. He wants to take what is most precious from the Lord; that is you and your sacred relationship. He wants you, he wants your family, he wants your relationships, and your security in Christ, so that he could accuse you before the Lord, disqualify you for the race, and render you ineffective for the Lord's Kingdom. Satan, parades himself like an Angel of light, blinding many well intended individuals, while other times appealing to ones own lust or pride, tempting and enticing them. While God will test what is in your heart to reveal weaknesses, Satan is the tempter who entices us, provoking us to act upon our frailty. We ought to surrender our hearts over to Jesus in genuine repentance, so not to be ensnared and deceived by Satan.

**James 1:13-15**

> When people are tempted, they should not say, "God is tempting me." Evil cannot tempt God, and God himself does not tempt anyone. But people are tempted when their own evil desire leads them away and traps them. This desire leads to sin, and then the sin grows and brings death. (NCV)

**1 Timothy 5:15**

> Some have in fact already turned away to follow Satan. (NIV)

**1 Corinthians 10:13**

> No temptation has seized you that isn't common for people. But God is faithful. He won't allow you to be tempted beyond your abilities. Instead, with the temptation, God will also supply a way out so that you will be able to endure it. (CEB)

Satan has laid traps for our loved ones to lure them by their own evil desires, because they are often the ones that Satan uses to snare us and keep us from fully walking in the light. The devil would steal your sons from you and bury them before their time, but our Lord Jesus, has made a way of escape that they should pass over them and escape from wickedness. We must set an example of moral, biblical standards before our children, by not cherishing the world or the things in the world and pray that we, together with our loved ones, will not be deceived or misled. Pray and ask that God's Word will always be in their heart. We must be diligent in praying for our loved ones, that they will be strong and vigorous to overcome the wicked one, the devil. We should pray that they will live to the divine will and purpose of the father and live a consistently, conscientious life and be righteous even as Jesus is righteous. No one has the love or compassion to pray for your loved ones like you do, so it is up to you to pray for them.

**Lamentations 2:19**

> Rise during the night and cry out. Pour out your hearts like water to the Lord. Lift up your hands to him in prayer, pleading for your children. (NLT)

**2 Timothy 2:26**

And that they may come to their senses and escape the snare of the devil, having been taken them captive by him to do his will. (NKJV)

**Titus 2:6-8**

In a similar way, urge the younger men to be self-restrained and to behave prudently [taking life seriously]. And show your own self in all respects to be a pattern and a model of good deeds and works, teaching what is unadulterated, showing gravity [having the strictest regard for truth and purity of motive], with dignity and seriousness. And let your instruction be sound and fit and wise and wholesome, vigorous and irrefutable and above censure, so that the opponent may be put to shame, finding nothing discrediting or evil to say about us. (AMP)

**Hebrews 2:14-15**

Since the children have flesh and blood, he too shared in their humanity so that by his death he might break the power of him who holds the power of death—that is, the devil—and free those who all their lives were held in slavery by their fear of death. (NIV)

**Psalm 144:11-14**

Save me! Rescue me from the power of my enemies. Their mouths are full of lies; they swear to tell the truth, but they lie instead. May our sons flourish in their youth like well-nurtured plants. May our daughters be like graceful pillars, carved to beautify a palace. May our barns be filled with crops of every kind. May the flocks in our fields multiply by the thousands, even tens of thousands, and may our oxen be loaded down with produce. May there be no enemy breaking through our walls, no going into captivity, no cries of alarm in our town squares. (NLT)

Ultimately, we need to see our precious family to the finish line, cheering them on, so that they enjoy perfect confidence, boldness and assurance for when the Lord Jesus appears at his coming, they do not shrink back. It is in Satan's interest to get us angry toward the Lord for being in these harsh situations and bitter toward life and God's people, in order to dismantle our best weapon - prayer. The Lord may choose not to operate on your behalf when you have unforgiveness in your heart and are heavy laden with sin. Justice will be driven back and righteousness will be far away from you. You will cry out, "Where is God?!" Truly, these are lonely times.

**Genesis 4:7**

> If you do well, will you not be accepted? And if you do not do well, sin is lurking at the door; its desire is for you, but you must master it." (NRSV)

**Psalm 42:3**

> My tears have been my food both day and night, as people constantly questioned me, "Where's your God now?" (CEB)

**Romans 16:20**

> And the God of peace will crush Satan under your feet shortly. The grace of our Lord Jesus Christ be with you. Amen (NKJV)

**Matthew 12:30**

> Anyone who isn't with me opposes me, and anyone who isn't working with me is actually working against me. (NLT)

**Mark 11:25**

> Whenever you stand up to pray, you must forgive what others have done to you. Then your Father in heaven will forgive your sins. (CEV)

**Ephesians 4:31-32**

> Put aside all bitterness, losing your temper, anger, shouting, and slander, along with every other evil. Be kind, compassionate, and forgiving to each other, in the same way God forgave you in Christ. (CEB)

Satan has a main strategy for stealing your joy and zest for life. Once he has alienated you from God and has you believe that no one else loves or cares about you, he will steal your relationships right out from beneath you.

Satan does not want us to enjoy the fellowship of family and community. I've heard people say, "I love God, I just don't love people." It seems people disappoint us sorely. Have you ever seen the worst behavior come out of even good people? Have you ever felt like you needed to expose them and show other people what they are really like? This is when the battle becomes a flesh battle instead of a spiritual battle. All people have their worst behavior and without proper nourishment of the relationship people can reveal some of their worst behaviors. When we try sizing up a person based on the fuel that Satan feeds us, that person will never measure up according to what we think is right. It is only through God's love can we truly love people and allow people to be imperfect.

Even though our lives are a process of glorification and will not be complete until we are in our glorified bodies, when Christ comes back again for us, it is important to know, that in his eyes, we are already a finished work. God see's perfection in each of his children and it is his desire that we see one another as he sees us and love one another as he loves us and not according to what we think others deserve.

**2 Corinthians 10:5**

> And we tear down every proud idea that raises itself against the knowledge of God. We also capture every thought and make it give up and obey Christ. (ERV)

**Matthew 22:36-39**

> Teacher, which is the great commandment in the Law?" And he said to him, "You shall love the Lord your God with all your heart and with all your soul and with all your mind. This is the great and first commandment. And a second is like it: You shall love your neighbor as yourself. (ESV)

**John 13:34-35**

> "Let me give you a new command: Love one another. In the same way I loved you, you love one another. This is how everyone will recognize that you are my disciples—when they see the love you have for each other." (MSG) The Message

**Matthew 12:25**

> However, knowing what they were thinking, Yeshua said to them, "Every kingdom divided against itself will be ruined,

and every city or household divided against itself will not survive. (CJB)

When we no longer enjoy relationships with our spouse, children, church or co-workers, Satan has stolen our joy. Some people enjoy pets more than the company of people. If people are so imperfect, then how do we enjoy each other? How do we find joy in loving one another? Outside of Christ we cannot truly love people. People require patience, unconditional and non-judgmental love. Only our Creator has the ability to love us the way we are. In order to have God's heart to be a stream of living water and a channel of love to other people, we need to stay close abiding in him. It is the Lord's spirit that empowers us to love others because being connected to people is such a big deal to God. God wants his family to be in unity and harmony.

Relationship is so important to God. The Father, the Son and the Holy Spirit are in relationship to one another.

Let us then learn to love people as they are in present, in order that family and community are healthy. We will enjoy people more when we realize that people belong to the Lord. God created all people, he loves them and they are his workmanship and not our own.

**John 15:4-6**

> Remain in me, and I will remain in you. For a branch cannot produce fruit if it is severed from the vine, and you cannot be fruitful unless you remain in me. "Yes, I am the vine; you are the branches. Those who remain in me, and I in them, will produce much fruit. For apart from me you can do nothing. Anyone who does not remain in me is thrown away like a useless branch and withers. Such branches are gathered into a pile to be burned. (NLT)

**John 7:38**

> Have faith in me, and you will have life-giving water flowing from deep inside you, just as the Scriptures say." (CEV)

**2 Corinthians 2:11**

> Lest Satan should take advantage of us; for we are not ignorant of his devices. (NKJV)

**Ephesians 2:10**

> For we are his workmanship, created in Christ Jesus for good works, which God prepared beforehand, that we should walk in them. (ESV)

**Acts 14:22**

> Strengthening the souls of the disciples, encouraging them to continue in the faith, and saying, "Through many tribulations we must enter the kingdom of God." (NASB)

# The World

If Satan, the "god of this world," could distract you by enticing you with the pleasures of the world, you will have lost your first love, *the Groom*. When suddenly, we have no time for God, because we are too busy pursuing our own will, we know we have left the Lord to find greener pastures. We will choose other pleasures over communion and obedience to God. When God doesn't seem to satisfy our soul any more we know that something else has taken center stage. The pleasures of the world are so temporal and can never quench the thirst of the soul - this too is another deception of Satan. Like the children of Israel looking back at Egypt they forgot they were slaves, instead they longed for Egypt's exotic way of life. The world will entice you and make you think it is your friend, especially when you are young and the world seems like a playground of opportunities.

However, the world will have your head spinning as it is never enough. You'll never be enough or have enough to fit in with the world because we are not part of the world. The world will never feel like home to you or I. So long as we pursue life in the world we will be unsatisfied. If you are looking for comfort in the things of the world and you Child belong to God, you will never feel the peaceful warmth of love and security as you do when you are in communion and obedience to

Jesus and the Holy Spirit. You will feel the Lord tugging at your heart calling you back to his heart. You will find that you can only go so far before you stop enjoying the world. You don't seem to get away with the things that others seem to get away with, this is because you do not belong to the world. The world is not your home and is not your destiny. You need to forsake the world; divorce the world and get back to your Kingdom citizenship.

**Matthew 10:22**

> Everyone will hate you on account of my name. But whoever stands firm until the end will be saved. (CEB)

**John 17:14**

> I have given and delivered to them Your word (message) and the world has hated them, because they are not of the world [do not belong to the world], just as I am not of the world. (AMP)

**1 John 2:15-17**

> Don't love this evil world or the things in it. If you love the world, you do not have the love of the Father in you. This is all there is in the world: wanting to please our sinful selves, wanting the sinful things we see, and being too proud of what we have. But none of these comes from the Father. They come from the world. The world is passing away, and all the things that people want in the world are passing away. But whoever does what God wants will live forever. (ERV)

**James 4:4-8**

> Adulterers and adulteresses! Do you not know that friendship with the world is enmity with God? Whoever therefore wants to be a friend of the world makes himself an enemy of God. Or do you think that the Scripture says in vain, "The Spirit who dwells in us yearns jealously"? (NKJV)

**Galatians 5:1**

> It was for freedom that Christ set us free; therefore keep standing firm and do not be subject again to a yoke of slavery. (NASB)

# Unequally Yoked

In 2 Corinthians 2:11, we are told not to be ignorant of Satan's devices so that he might take advantage of us. Satan is the stark contrast between the light of Christ and the dark kingdom. Satan's kingdom is in darkness and his captives are in blindness and they cannot understand the light (John 1:5).

We are warned not to join ourselves in serious relationship with people who are not yet of the Kingdom of God. This is not to say that we do not have friendships with people that are not believers. While we must recognize that God sees all people as his children, many will reject him.

Typically it is not wise to enter into marriage with someone who is not yet embracing the Kingdom of God, nor do we participate in their way of lifestyle. Since it is not possible for a non-saved person to think with the mind of Christ they will have a different view on life, where they want to go and how they want to get there. Should you find yourself in this relationship you will find yourself being pulled in a different and contrasting direction. Contention will be at an all time high and you will not experience the peace of God without his intervention.

**Exodus 34:12**

Be careful that you don't make a covenant with the inhabitants of the land to which you are going, or it will become a dangerous trap for you. (CEB)

**Jude 1:18-19**

They said to you, "In the end time scoffers will come living according to their own ungodly desires." These people create divisions. Since they don't have the Spirit, they are worldly. (CEB)

**2 Corinthians 6:14**

You are not the same as those who don't believe. So don't join yourselves to them. Good and evil don't belong together. Light and darkness cannot share the same room. (ERV)

**James 3:11**

Can both fresh water and salt water flow from the same spring? (NIV)

**2 Timothy 3:1-5**

But mark this: There will be terrible times in the last days. People will be lovers of themselves, lovers of money, boastful, proud, abusive, disobedient to their parents, ungrateful, unholy, without love, unforgiving, slanderous, without self-control, brutal, not lovers of the good, treacherous, rash, conceited, lovers of pleasure rather than lovers of God — having a form of godliness but denying its power. Have nothing to do with such people. (NIV)

**1 Corinthians 2:11-14, 16**

No one knows the thoughts of God except the Spirit of God. Now we did not receive the spirit of the world, but we received the Spirit that is from God so that we can know all that God has given us. And we speak about these things, not with words taught us by human wisdom but with words taught us by the Spirit. And so we explain spiritual truths to spiritual people. A person who does not have the Spirit does not accept the truths that come from the Spirit of God. That person thinks they are foolish and cannot understand them, because they can only be judged to be true by the Spirit.... But we have the mind of Christ. (NCV)

**1 John 1:7**

But if we live in the light, as God does, we share in life with each other. And the blood of his Son Jesus washes all our sins away. (CEV)

**1 Thessalonians 5:5-8**

All of you are children of light and children of the day. We don't belong to night or darkness. So then, let's not sleep like the others, but let's stay awake and stay sober. People who sleep sleep at night, and people who get drunk get drunk at night. Since we belong to the day, let's stay sober, wearing faithfulness and love as a piece of armor that protects our body and the hope of salvation as a helmet. (CEB)

**Psalm 120:6**

I have spent too much time living among people who hate peace. (CEV)

**Psalm 120:7**

I ask for peace, but they want war. (ERV)

**Psalm 122:8**

For the sake of my brothers and my friends, I will now say, "May peace be within you." (NASB)

# Empty Wells

The Samaritan woman came to the well every day to fill her water jar but because of her shame, she did not come when the other women would normally come. While the respectable women would fill their jars up at the early hour or in the evening, when the sun was not as hot, this Samaritan woman would come in the heat of the noonday in order to avoid the other women. Her shame caused her to avoid the other women, but Jesus took notice of her. You can read about her in John chapter 4 of the Bible. While the others saw a woman of promiscuity, Jesus saw a thirsty and hungry soul. Jesus knew that she had five husbands, but Jesus saw her heart. Jesus did not come to condemn her, but to restore her. It is the world that leaves you empty and unsatisfied. It is the world that condemns us.

Like this Samaritan woman some of us will try to fill our lives with empty relationships, when one after the other we find they were not what we were really searching for at all. We gave all we could and it was never enough. Only Jesus has the well spring of life that truly satisfies our soul. When we have no more regard for this life, because we realize that life's been wasted chasing shallow dreams and hiding behind religion, you will willfully lay your life down.

**Isaiah 12:3**

Therefore with joy will you draw water from the wells of salvation. (AMP)

**John 4:14**

But those who drink the water I give will never be thirsty again. It becomes a fresh, bubbling spring within them, giving them eternal life." (NLT)

**Isaiah 58:11**

The LORD will guide you always; he will satisfy your needs in a sun-scorched land and will strengthen your frame. You will be like a well-watered garden, like a spring whose waters never fail. (NIV)

**Matthew 6:33**

Seek first the kingdom of God and His righteousness, and then all these things will be given to you too. (VOICE)

**John 3:17-18**

For God sent the Son into the world, not to condemn the world, but that the world might be saved through him. He who believes in him is not condemned; he who does not believe is condemned already, because he has not believed in the name of the only Son of God. (RSV)

**Matthew 10:39**

If you cling to your life, you will lose it; but if you give up your life for me, you will find it. (NLT)

# The Flesh

If Satan can distract you by enticing you with pleasures of the flesh, like indulgences, obsessions, and perversities, you will have polluted yourself and disqualified yourself as a soul winner and witness in this world. The apostle Paul said to the church at Corinthians, these are the works of the flesh: lust, idols, fornication, tempting the Lord and murmuring against the Lord, upon which the ends of the world are come.

If you need a substance to self medicate yourself each morning in order to cope with this life, rather than looking to your Savior, you have a false god and have been deceived.

For example, Lot's daughters had been deceived when they distorted reality. Lot led his daughters into Sodom and had educated them in the culture of Sodom and their behavior was a direct result of their spiritual condition. The daughters of Lot thought their father was the only man left on earth. Lot's daughters didn't look to God to solve their problem. They simply came to their own immoral, irrational decision, caused by their oppressive thoughts. If you are familiar with this story, you know how twisted and perverted their thinking had become.

**Genesis 18:20-21**

Then the LORD said, "The outcry against Sodom and Gomorrah is so great and their sin so grievous that I will go down and see if what they have done is as bad as the outcry that has reached me. If not, I will know." (NIV)

**2 Peter 2:5-9**

If he did not spare the ancient world, but preserved Noah, a herald of righteousness, with seven others, when he brought a flood upon the world of the ungodly; if by turning the cities of Sodom and Gomorrah to ashes he condemned them to extinction, making them an example of what is going to happen to the ungodly; and if he rescued righteous Lot, greatly distressed by the sensual conduct of the wicked (for as that righteous man lived among them day after day, he was tormenting his righteous soul over their lawless deeds that he saw and heard); then the Lord knows how to rescue the godly from trials, and to keep the unrighteous under punishment until the day of judgment. (ESV)

**James 1:14**

But each one is tempted when he is drawn away by his own desires and enticed. (NKJV)

**1 Peter 2:11**

Beloved, I implore you as aliens and strangers and exiles [in this world] to abstain from the sensual urges (the evil desires, the passions of the flesh, your lower nature) that wage war against the soul. (AMP)

**Colossians 2:14**

> He canceled the record of the charges against us and took it
> away by nailing it to the cross. (NLT)

War is necessary when we need to purge out the wickedness of the
world. War with the flesh is imminent when there is a moral decadence.
Yes, Jesus died to set us free from the sin and captivity that leads to
death, but we need to fight the desires for sins that keep us from living
moral lives, as though we were still in captivity - as though we have
no king. When Israel had no king, everyone did as he saw fit. This is
the way people of the world live, without King Jesus living in their
heart. The battles are necessary for the process of sanctification, as we
are being made holy - resulting in a changed life-style, equipped for
kingdom living.

Therefore, we need not live the lifestyle of the people of the world.
We must remember we are strangers in the world. We are a special
people and a holy priesthood.

**Judges 21:25**

> In those days there was no king in Israel; all the people did
> what was right in their own eyes. (NRSV)

**Jude 1:18-19**

> They told you that in the last times there would be scoffers
> whose purpose in life is to satisfy their ungodly desires.
> These people are the ones who are creating divisions among
> you. They follow their natural instincts because they do not
> have God's Spirit in them. (NLT)

**Ephesians 2:1-3**

In the past you were spiritually dead because of your sins and the things you did against God. Yes, in the past your lives were full of those sins. You lived the way the world lives, following the ruler of the evil powers that are above the earth. That same spirit is now working in those who refuse to obey God. In the past all of us lived like that, trying to please our sinful selves. We did all the things our bodies and minds wanted. Like everyone else in the world, we deserved to suffer God's anger just because of the way we were. (ERV)

**Proverbs 19:20-21**

Listen to counsel and accept discipline, that you may be wise the rest of your days. (NASB)

**1 Peter 2:9**

But you are his chosen people, the King's priests. You are a holy nation, people who belong to God. He chose you to tell about the wonderful things he has done. He brought you out of the darkness of sin into his wonderful light. (ERV)

# Surrendered

Before experiencing the blessings of the Promised Land, which is your spiritual breakthrough and your victory, it is essential to deal with the flesh. The flesh-man is that sin nature that you were born into. It is not the spirit-man that you receive when you are redeemed (born-again). The flesh nature does what is contrary to the work of the Spirit. It is the sinful nature. The flesh must be circumcised (Joshua 5). Heat is used for the refining of precious metals to burn away impurities. When the trials of suffering begin to apply heat to our lives, it begins to purge out all the chaff and debris of the world. When this happens, you will feel as though you are dying. Mentally and emotionally you feel a sense of loss, as in death, and the grieving begins. Grieving for all personal losses, such as lost time, the loss of relationships and the loss of opportunities.

When my marriage hit a road block after fifteen years of marriage, I felt as though I was put on the sacrificial table and cut into a thousand pieces. My dreams represented broken glass, as in this dream, I dreamed many years ago. I was being carried by the Lord Jesus over a field of broken glass and I sensed the presence of his genuine love for me as the Lord carried me in his arms over the field of broken glass. Even though my prior dreams seemed dead, I knew that the Lord would have a new dream for me; out of darkness would come light. Although not ready to dream again, I knew that the Lord would ask me to dream boldly. Like an expectant mother, I anticipate the joy of delivery.

**Isaiah 64:8**

> But now, O Lord, You are our Father, We are the clay, and You our potter; And all of us are the work of Your hand. (NASB)

**Ezekiel 24:11**

> Then set the empty pot on the coals till it becomes hot and its copper glows, so that its impurities may be melted and its deposit burned away. (NIV)

**Isaiah 45:9**

> Woe to him who strives with his Maker an earthern vessel with the potter. Does the clay say to him who fashions it, 'What are you making?' or 'Your work has no handles'? (RSV)

**Lamentations 3:40**

> Let us examine and see what we have done and then return to the Lord. (NCV)

**Hebrews 12:11**

> We do not enjoy being disciplined. It is painful at the time, but later, after we have learned from it, we have peace, because we start living in the right way. (NCV)

**Lamentations 3:31-32**

For the Lord will not cast off for ever: But though he cause grief, yet will he have compassion according to the multitude of his mercies. (KJV)

# The Soldier Dies

We are prone to sin when we walk in our flesh and our feet are swift to rush to it. If it were not for God's wonderful grace of Christ, none of us would remain faithful. Until we are sick and tired of the cycle of war-life we will never get off the cycle to be still and know God. We will continue wandering in the cycle of disappointment. These parched and dry times are to help us thirst for God more and learn obedience even to death - death to self.

It is necessary to die, in order to produce life. Like a seed, we never really remain dead; a seed can lie dormant, sometimes for many years. When we have gifts of God, yet allow our gifts to lie dormant, it serves no value to the Kingdom of God. Inside that seed is an embryo waiting for life. In that seed is DNA that can only reproduce exactly what it was intended to be! That means that if you are a Christian, that genetic material in that seed is going to produce a "Little Christ." But don't expect to be loved and accepted by this world. Like Jesus Christ, we are led to the cross of calvary to lay down our lives. It is the cross that leads us to his heart. At the cross of calvary we find resurrection power.

**John 12:24**

I tell you the truth, unless a kernel of wheat is planted in the soil and dies, it remains alone. But its death will produce many new kernels—a plentiful harvest of new lives. (NLT)

**Psalm 107:14**

He brought them out of darkness and the shadow of death, and broke their chains in pieces. (NKJV)

**Lamentations 3:55-58**

Lord, I called your name from the bottom of the pit. You heard my voice. You didn't close your ears. You didn't refuse to rescue me. You came to me on the day that I called out to you. You said to me, "Don't be afraid." You defended me and brought me back to life. (ERV)

**2 Corinthians 4:10-12**

We always carry around in our body the death of Jesus, so that the life of Jesus may also be revealed in our body. For we who are alive are always being given over to death for Jesus' sake, so that his life may also be revealed in our mortal body. So then, death is at work in us, but life is at work in you. (NIV)

**2 Corinthians 4:14-15**

We know that God, who raised the Lord Jesus, will also raise us with Jesus and present us to himself together with you. All of this is for your benefit. And as God's grace reaches more and more people, there will be great thanksgiving, and God will receive more and more glory. (NLT)

**John 12:27**

Now My soul is troubled and distressed, and what shall I say? Father, save Me from this hour [of trial and agony]? But it was for this very purpose that I have come to this hour [that I might undergo it]. (AMP)

**Colossians 3:9-10**

Don't lie to each other. You have taken off those old clothes— the person you once were and the bad things you did then. Now you are wearing a new life, a life that is new every day. You are growing in your understanding of the one who made you. You are becoming more and more like him. (ERV)

**Colossians 1:6**

In the same way, the gospel is bearing fruit and growing throughout the whole world just as it has been doing among you since the day you heard it and truly understood God's grace. (NIV)

**Hebrews 4:16**

So let us come boldly to the throne of our gracious God. There we will receive his mercy, and we will find grace to help us when we need it most. (NLT)

# Cross of Calvary

Knowing God to a deeper level will require that we first die, for when a person loses the fear of death they are ready to move into new realms of impact. It takes courage to lay down your life. Every Christian is led to the cross of Jesus but we are not left at the cross.

Yet by his resurrection power, you will rise again with relief and deliverance, just as he did, endowed with power from the Holy Spirit. You will arise ready to turn your heart completely over to Him to live your God-given purpose and destiny.

Having been trained and disciplined by the battles you will experience a new level of peace and serenity you've never known - the harvest season of Fall. Get ready for the blessings to come forth.

**Psalm 71:20-21**

> You have allowed me to suffer much hardship, but you will restore me to life again and lift me up from the depths of the earth. You will restore me to even greater honor and comfort me once again. (NLT)

**Romans 14:9**

The reason Christ died and rose from the dead to live again was so he would be Lord over both the dead and the living. (NCV)

**Joel 2:28**

And afterward I will pour out My Spirit upon all flesh; and your sons and your daughters shall prophesy, your old men shall dream dreams, your young men shall see visions. (AMP)

**Genesis 28:15**

"I am with you, and I will protect you everywhere you go. I will bring you back to this land. I will not leave you until I have done what I have promised." (ERV)

**2 Corinthians 4:17**

For our light and momentary troubles are achieving for us an eternal glory that far outweighs them all. (NIV)

**John 5:24**

"I tell you the truth, those who listen to my message and believe in God who sent me have eternal life. They will never be condemned for their sins, but they have already passed from death into life. (NLT)

**Acts 2:39-41**

This promise is for you, your children, and for all who are far away—as many as the Lord our God invites." With many other words he testified to them and encouraged them, saying, "Be saved from this perverse generation." Those who accepted Peter's message were baptized. God brought about three thousand people into the community on that day. (CEB)

**Psalm 118:17**

I will live and not die, and I will tell what the Lord has done. (ERV)

# THE CHILD

# It's a New Day

Fall is that season when all the smells remind us of all the comfort foods we enjoyed as a child. The child is playful as the noon day and carefree, running through the pile of raked leaves, the deadness of summer behind her. The patience in suffering now yielding its crop. Out emerges, not the newly babe child, yet a more mature child. The child who has been nurtured underneath the wings of protection of the Father is now fully trained in the scriptures. She has pursued peace and her God alone. She has complete confidence in her salvation. The child knows the world is a dangerous place and has learned how to shelter and rest in the father's arms. The Father is pleased by her willingness to pursue his will instead of her own. She is willing to let the Father lead. It is his desire that she continually abide in him, because by obeying and remaining, she is assured a place of safety. For any evil that comes against her will have to first, go through the Father.

She must remain, close at camp, until she is healed of every wound.

**James 5:7**

> See how the farmer waits for the land to yield its valuable crop,
> patiently waiting for the autumn and spring rains. (NIV)

**Ecclesiastes 3:1**

There is a time for everything, and everything on earth has its special season. (NCV)

**Psalm 91:1-4**

He who dwells in the secret place of the Most High. Shall abide under the shadow of the Almighty. I will say of the Lord, "He is my refuge and my fortress; My God, in Him I will trust." Surely He shall deliver you from the snare of the fowler and from the perilous pestilence. He shall cover you with His feathers, and under His wings you shall take refuge; His truth shall be your shield and buckler. (NKJV)

**Deuteronomy 11:14**

Then I will give you the rain for your land in its season, the early rain and the latter rain, that you may gather in your grain, your new wine, and your oil. (NKJV)

**Ephesians 4:14**

No prolonged infancies among us, please. We'll not tolerate babes in the woods, small children who are an easy mark for impostors. God wants us to grow up, to know the whole truth and tell it in love—like Christ in everything. We take our lead from Christ, who is the source of everything we do. He keeps us in step with each other. His very breath and blood flow through us, nourishing us so that we will grow up healthy in God, robust in love. (MSG)

**Isaiah 28:9**

"Who is it he is trying to teach? To whom is he explaining his message? To children weaned from their milk, to those just taken from the breast? (NIV)

**Romans 15:4**

Everything that was written in the past was written to teach us. Those things were written so that we could have hope. That hope comes from the patience and encouragement that the Scriptures give us. (ERV)

**Luke 6:40**

The student is not above the teacher, but everyone who is fully trained will be like their teacher. (NIV)

**Hebrews 5:8**

Jesus is God's own Son, but still he had to suffer before he could learn what it really means to obey God. (CEV)

**Hebrews 5:14**

Solid food is for those who are mature, who through training have the skill to recognize the difference between right and wrong. (NLT)

**Hebrews 6:1**

So let us stop going over the basic teachings about Christ again and again. Let us go on instead and become mature in our understanding. Surely we don't need to start again with the fundamental importance of repenting from evil deeds and placing our faith in God. (NLT)

# The Father's Amazing Love

Many years ago I attended a Women's Retreat. I remember the speaker clearly as she referred to the Father as, "Abba," and "Daddy," many times in her talk. I went home bothered in my spirit, although, I wasn't quite sure why. I knew that the Lord was our Father and Creator, and I knew that "Abba" was an affectionate term, like our English word, "Daddy." Yet I was a little uncomfortable with her title reference to the *Holy* Father. Then one day, it occurred to me that this woman was experiencing another season, besides the *Bride* and the *Warrior*. Up to then, I did not know any other seasons of life. I knew then that the Lord was showing me a new place in him. I began to want to know Abba-Daddy. This woman had an intimacy with the Father and a glow about her that I immediately began to covet. I recognized how comfortable she was with the Father and how she resonated with confidence. I wanted to be able to climb on top of Abba-Daddy's lap and look in his gentle eyes, and know that he was truly pleased with me. Hope began to rise inside me.

Studies have proven that a child simply cannot thrive without love. The Child must grasp the truth that she is extremely valued by the Father and that He loves her with an amazing, everlasting, unconditional love.

Since this time I was amazed to discover new revelations of his magnificent character. This new discovery of the Father's love was not entirely new, however, there was a new depth to my understanding. The scriptures I knew and read many times before were becoming more alive to me. I was also learning that the Father's love is personal and real and more importantly, there was nothing I could do, or not do, to mess it up.

I discovered that I was the one lost sheep out of the ninety-nine and that the Lord Jesus, would search for me until I was found. I was the Prodigal Child who left home and squandered my inheritance, no longer worthy to be called his child, yet he will celebrate my homecoming with celebration and feasting (Luke 15). Because I belong to him and he bought and paid the full price for me, he will seal me with his Holy Spirit. He will keep me until the day of Redemption, when he shall return again and nothing will be able to snatch me from his loving arms. This thought assures me of the fact that I am safe and secure in my salvation. I do not have to work for it and I cannot lose it.

Even more amazing, is that he, the Father would send his Son, in the flesh, to the Earth to suffer for my sins. Jesus would leave His perfect home, a place where there is no sickness, disease or sorrow, to become a stranger in this world, to be rejected, persecuted and die for me. In understanding his love is eternal and unchanging we are spurred on with greater devotion to learn the authentic walk.

**Psalm 63:7-8**

> Because You have been my help, therefore in the shadow of your wings I will rejoice. My soul follows close behind you; your right hand upholds me. (NKJV)

**Matthew 18:3**

> Truly, I say to you, unless you turn and become like children, you will never enter the kingdom of heaven. (ESV)

**Romans 8:15-16**

So you have not received a spirit that makes you fearful slaves. Instead, you received God's Spirit when he adopted you as his own children. Now we call him, "Abba, Father." For his Spirit joins with our spirit to affirm that we are God's children. (NLT)

**Romans 8:35**

Can anything separate us from the love Christ has for us? Can troubles or problems or sufferings or hunger or nakedness or danger or violent death? (NCV)

**Romans 8:39**

Nor height, nor depth, nor any other created thing, will be able to separate us from the love of God, which is in Christ Jesus our Lord. (NASB)

**Ephesians 4:30**

Do not grieve the Holy Spirit of God, by whom you were sealed for the day of redemption. (NASB)

**John 10:28-29**

I give them eternal life, and they will never perish, and no one will snatch them out of my hand. My Father, who has given them to me, is greater than all, and no one is able to snatch them out of the Father's hand. (ESV)

**1 Corinthians 6:20**

> You have been purchased at a great price, so use your body to bring glory to God! (VOICE)

**1 John 4:10**

> This is real love—not that we loved God, but that he loved us and sent his Son as a sacrifice to take away our sins. (NLT)

# *Kingdom of God*

Children typically trust and depend on their parents to supply all their needs; such is the Kingdom of God. Unless we become like children and trust and depend completely on God we cannot enter the Kingdom of God. The Kingdom of God is one of righteousness, joy and peace. These are attributes we desire but often have a difficult time possessing because we tend to want to take charge and take over the driver's wheel. Two things we don't understand about God, one is his timing and the other is his purpose. We will misunderstand the purpose and often rush the process if we are anxious, thereby not living in our true destiny. Children may tire easily and must be led by the hand so not to give up.

The Promise Land was beyond Jordan. But one of Israel's tribes felt that their needs were already satisfied East of the Jordan. They would choose not to make their home in the land of Canaan, *the promise land*. To never fulfill your true destiny is to merely settle with complacency and many are not even happy at that.

However, what unspeakable joy come to them that see the blessings of the promise fulfilled. The gift of abundant life and eternal life are the very essence of the gospel. When I was wounded, in the season of the *Warrior*, I knew that if I would persevere, God would deliver me through the times of suffering and pain, but I wanted my deliverance instantly. I wanted to rush the process and get to the "Joy, that cometh in the morning." When tragedies come into our lives, like a death, critical illness of a loved one, or divorce, it is hard to understand God's purpose in the crux of the situation. We question why a loving God would allow such things. God, being sovereign, deals with issues of the heart that we are not even aware of for the long-term purpose. The long-term purpose being to free us from our fear and captivities, in order to give us a freedom to live a more abundant life. But because we misunderstand God's purpose, or do not see the complete picture, we allow our flesh nature to take over the driver's wheel. Taking control only delays the process.

Complete love and trust is what Abba-Daddy desires from us. A child may not have the ability to understand principles that are beyond her, but she must trust the love of the parent to care for her needs. God will provide and he will deliver according to every promise he has spoken. Our job is, simply to activate our faith and believe, irregardless of the circumstances, in doing so, such is the Kingdom of God.

**John 3:3**

> Jesus answered, "I tell you the truth, unless you are born again, you cannot be in God's kingdom." (NCV)

**Mark 4:11**

> And he said unto them, unto you it is given to know the mystery of the kingdom of God: but unto them that are without, all these things are done in parables: (KJV)

**Matthew 7:11**

> If you, then, who are evil, know how to give good gifts to your children, how much more will your Father who is in heaven give good gifts to those who ask him! (ESV)

**Isaiah 30:15**

In quietness and trust is your strength. (NIV)

**Psalm 36:7**

How precious is Your lovingkindness, O God! Therefore the children of men put their trust under the shadow of Your wings. (NKJV)

**Isaiah 30:18**

So the Lord must wait for you to come to him so he can show you his love and compassion. For the Lord is a faithful God. Blessed are those who wait for his help. (NLT)

# Love Falls Like Rain

Joy emerges with a deep trust and gratefulness for all that the Father is. No longer is obedience work and turmoil. What was once difficult is now lighter, because her trust and faith have been made deeper. You Child are forging on; you are pressing on. You shall see the Promises. With renewed determination, there will be no turning back.

It is not that the Child no longer experiences the battles, but the Child, having been tested and tried through the struggles of life, fully trusts in her Savior. Trust is the safety net for the believer. No longer will she waiver or doubt when she prays and asks for deliverance, for she knows that being double-minded only prolongs the battle. She now realizes that double mindedness is fruitlessness. She will make all her request known to her Lord and she will rest assured that he will fight all her battles. No longer is she the woman she used to be. She will stand confident in her new transformed life.

Love falls down like the rain, it refreshes the soul.

**Psalm 1:1-3**

> God blesses those people who refuse evil advice and won't
> follow sinners or join in sneering at God. Instead, the Law

of the Lord makes them happy, and they think about it day and night. They are like trees growing beside a stream, trees that produce fruit in season and always have leaves. Those people succeed in everything they do. (CEV)

**Ezekiel 29:16**

Egypt will no longer be a source of confidence for the people of Israel but will be a reminder of their sin in turning to her for help. Then they will know that I am the Sovereign LORD.'" (NIV)

**Psalm 27:3-4**

Even if an army gathers against me, my heart will not be afraid. Even if war rises against me, I will be sure of You. One thing I have asked from the Lord, that I will look for: that I may live in the house of the Lord all the days of my life, to look upon the beauty of the Lord, and to worship in His holy house. (NLV)

**James 1:2-8**

Dear brothers and sisters, when troubles come your way, consider it an opportunity for great joy. For you know that when your faith is tested, your endurance has a chance to grow. So let it grow, for when your endurance is fully developed, you will be perfect and complete, needing nothing. If you need wisdom, ask our generous God, and he will give it to you. He will not rebuke you for asking. But when you ask him, be sure that your faith is in God alone. Do not waver, for a person with divided loyalty is as unsettled as a wave of the sea that is blown and tossed by the wind. Such people should not expect to receive anything from the Lord. Their loyalty is divided between God and the world, and they are unstable in everything they do. (NLT)

**Ephesians 4:14**

As a result, we are no longer to be children, tossed here and there by waves and carried about by every wind of doctrine, by the trickery of men, by craftiness in deceitful scheming; (NASB)

**Psalm 27:13-14**

Yet I am confident I will see the Lord's goodness while I am here in the land of the living. Wait patiently for the Lord. Be brave and courageous. Yes, wait patiently for the Lord. (NLT)

# Voice of the Wind

Once you press in, allowing God to open the eyes of your heart, you are ready to hear clearly the voice of the Father. The Child listens to the Lord's instructions, even when she knows not where she is being led. The children of Israel, while in the desert, did not know where they were being led. Now able to be still and incline her ear and listen to instruction, the Lord, who is wonderful in counsel and magnificent in wisdom, has much to teach the Child. The Child has new ears. The Father will ask, "Walk with me child."

Israel had waited many years for this time, to leave their unfaithful hearts behind and recognize their true, *Royal* identity. No more wandering, no more looking to the left or to the right. The Child now enjoys the fruit of the harvest that is evident of her faith in him. Her reproach has been broken off and the Lord is ready to drive out her enemies. The enemy comes to steal what belongs in the house. But the enemy must be bound first, in order that the house be set in order. These are the powers that must be dealt with and when they are, you can be sure the Lord will ask you to advance.

**Mark 4:9**

Then Jesus said, "Let those with ears use them and listen!" (NCV)

**Psalm 37:23-24**

The Lord directs the steps of the godly. He delights in every detail of their lives. Though they stumble, they will never fall, for the Lord holds them by the hand. (NLT)

**Numbers 9:15-18**

On the day the Holy Tent, the Tent of the Agreement, was set up, a cloud covered it. At night the cloud over the Holy Tent looked like fire. The cloud stayed over the Holy Tent all the time. And at night the cloud looked like fire. When the cloud moved from its place over the Holy Tent, the Israelites followed it. When the cloud stopped, that is the place where the Israelites camped. This was the way the Lord showed the Israelites when to move and when to stop and set up camp. While the cloud stayed over the Holy Tent, the people continued to camp in that same place. (ERV)

**John 10:4-5**

When he has brought out all his own, he goes on ahead of them, and his sheep follow him because they know his voice. But they will never follow a stranger; in fact, they will run away from him because they do not recognize a stranger's voice." (NIV)

**Joshua 6:10**

"Do not give a war cry, do not raise your voices, do not say a word until the day I tell you to shout. Then shout!" (NIV)

**Isaiah 30:20-21**

And though the Lord give you the bread of adversity, and the water of affliction, yet shall not thy teachers be removed into a corner any more, but thine eyes shall see thy teachers: and thine ears shall hear a word behind thee, saying, This is the way, walk ye in it, when ye turn to the right hand, and when ye turn to the left. (KJV)

**Isaiah 58:13-14**

If you honor it by not going your own way and not doing as you please or speaking idle words, then you will find your joy in the LORD. (NIV)

**Proverbs 8:33-35**

Hear instruction and be wise, and do not neglect it. Blessed is the one who listens to me, watching daily at my gates, waiting beside my doors. For whoever finds me finds life and obtains favor from the Lord. (ESV)

**Proverbs 1:23**

Come and listen to my counsel. I'll share my heart with you and make you wise. (NLT)

**Proverbs 2:3-4**

> Ask for good judgment. Cry out for understanding. Look for wisdom like silver. Search for it like hidden treasure. (ERV)

**Psalm 85:8**

> I listen carefully to what God the LORD is saying, for he speaks peace to his faithful people. But let them not return to their foolish ways. (NLT)

**Isaiah 56:1**

> This is what the LORD says: "Be just and fair to all. Do what is right and good, for I am coming soon to rescue you and to display my righteousness among you. (NLT)

**Jeremiah 33:3**

> 'Call to Me, and I will answer you, and show you great and mighty things, which you do not know.' (NKJV)

# "Resurrect My Child"

Having sat in the Lord's presence, fully surrendered and spiritually alive, after a long spiritual slumber, the *Warrior* becomes the *Child*. With renewed commitment and dedication, from death to life, the child arises from the dust to lay hold of new life the Lord has given. It is the Child who must slay Goliath and declare glory. Speak and declare the word of promises to your shattered and broken life, your fears of failure, fears of rejection, fears of love and broken dreams. Break every chain of bondage that comes from the weight of guilt, shame and fear. Break off the shackles of loneliness and abandonment. Speak life in your present. Speak life to your future.

And now, get ready to advance! Awaken and see that nothing is impossible for our God!

**Ephesians 5:14**

> "Wake up, sleeper, rise from the dead, and Christ will shine on you." (NIV)

**Judges 5:12**

'Wake up, wake up, Deborah! Wake up, wake up, break out in song! Arise (NIV)

**Isaiah 43:19**

See, I am doing a new thing! Now it springs up; do you not perceive it? I am making a way in the wilderness and streams in the wasteland. (NIV)

**Ezekiel 37:3-5**

He said to me, "Son of man, can these bones live?" I answered, "O Lord God, only You know that." He said to me, "Speak in My name over these bones. Say to them, 'O dry bones, hear the Word of the Lord.' This is what the Lord God says to these bones: 'I will make breath come into you, and you will come to life. (NLV)

**Isaiah 26:19**

But the Lord says, "Your people have died, but they will live again. The bodies of my people will rise from death. Dead people in the ground, stand and be happy! The dew covering you is like the dew sparkling in the light of a new day. It shows that a new time is coming, when the earth will give birth to the dead who are in it." (ERV)

**Ezra 9:9**

He has granted us new life to rebuild the house of our God and repair its ruins. (NIV)

**Isaiah 42:13**

The LORD will march out like a champion, like a warrior he will stir up his zeal; with a shout he will raise the battle cry and will triumph over his enemies. (NIV)

**Zechariah 2:8**

For the Lord of All says, "The Lord of shining-greatness has sent Me against the nations which have robbed you in battle. For whoever touches you, touches what is of great worth to Him. (NLV)

# The Jordan River

It was the children of the faithless generation that was ready to go to war as true Warriors and Conquerors (Joshua 3). Jericho was the first city that was conquered in the Promise Land - this made way for the Children of Israel to go in and take the land that God had promised them. The Jordan River, where they crossed over to get to Jericho, marked their decision to forge forward. This marks the spot where they had stepped over the line and they would not turn back, compromise, be lured back or be still. It is here that they step into the promises of the Word.

Free from bondage, the Lord leads the Child by the hand, teaching the Child a new walk, a new talk and a new song. The Child sits in quietness and waits upon the Lord. Humbly the Child awaits the rescue. Because the Child is in obedience it enables the Lord to bless. He no longer restrains himself. The Lord shields the Child from danger. The Lord fights the battle and leads her safely to higher grounds.

This is it, the moment in time, when you know what you must do. No longer are you inhibited by not recognizing the Father's voice. You have been trained in the ashes of adversity. With your future goal in mind you will plunge forward, even unto the unknown.

### Deuteronomy 11:11

But the land that you will soon cross the Jordan River to take is a land of hills and valleys, a land that drinks rain from heaven. (NCV)

### Isaiah 58:9-10

Then you shall call, and the Lord will answer; you shall cry, and he will say, 'Here I am.' If you take away the yoke from your midst, the pointing of the finger, and speaking wickedness, if you pour yourself out for the hungry and satisfy the desire of the afflicted, then shall your light rise in the darkness and your gloom be as the noonday. (ESV)

### Psalm 95:6-7

Come, let us worship and bow down, let us kneel before the Lord our Maker. For He is our God, and we are the people of His pasture and the sheep of His hand. (NASB)

### Deuteronomy 31:13

Since their children do not know this law, they must hear it. They must learn to respect the Lord your God for as long as they live in the land you are crossing the Jordan River to take for your own. (NCV)

### Deuteronomy 6:1-6

These are the commands, decrees and laws the LORD your God directed me to teach you to observe in the land that you are crossing the Jordan to possess, so that you, your children and their children after them may fear the LORD your God as long as you live by keeping all his decrees and commands that I give you, and so that you may enjoy long life. Hear, Israel, and be careful to obey so that it may go well with you and that you may increase greatly in a land flowing with milk and honey, just as the LORD, the God of your ancestors, promised you.

Hear, O Israel: The LORD our God, the LORD is one. Love the LORD your God with all your heart and with all your soul and with all your

strength. These commandments that I give you today are to be on your hearts. (NIV)

**Joshua 1:7**

Only be strong and very courageous, that you may observe to do according to all the law which Moses my servant commanded you; do not turn from it to the right hand or to the left, that you may prosper wherever you go. (NKJV)

**Joshua 7:12**

Destroy whatever among you is devoted to destruction. (NIV)

**Isaiah 58:14**

I will cause you to ride in triumph on the heights of the land and to feast on the inheritance of your father Jacob." For the mouth of the LORD has spoken. (NIV)

# The Fruits of Righteousness

There is no greater joy than for a Child of the Light to walk in step with the Spirit of the Father. The Children of the Light will no longer continue to walk in sin and darkness. The Children of the Light will not continue to stumble and fall, because they know the Father's heart. You Child are the apple of His eye because you are fully devoted to Him. You will put on your true self, which is like God, in righteousness and holiness. The Father is pleased when your desire is to be as He is - Holy.

**3 John 1:3-4**

> It gave me great joy when some believers came and testified about your faithfulness to the truth, telling how you continue to walk in it. I have no greater joy than to hear that my children are walking in the truth. (NIV)

**Psalm 37:23-24**

> The steps of a man are established by the Lord, when he delights in his way; though he fall, he shall not be cast headlong, for the Lord upholds his hand. (ESV)

**Jeremiah 29:14**

I will be found by you," says the Lord. "I will end your captivity and restore your fortunes. I will gather you out of the nations where I sent you and will bring you home again to your own land." (NLT)

**Deuteronomy 7:13**

He will love you, bless you, and multiply you. He will also bless the fruit of your womb and the fruit of your ground, your grain and your wine and your oil, the increase of your herds and the young of your flock, in the land that he swore to your fathers to give you. (ESV)

**2 Samuel 23:2-4**

The Lord's Spirit spoke through me. His word was on my tongue. The God of Israel spoke. The Rock of Israel said to me, 'Whoever rules people fairly, who rules with respect for God, is like the morning light at dawn, like a morning without clouds. He is like sunshine after a rain that makes tender grass grow from the ground.' (ERV)

# Treasures in the Storehouse

Imagine you were wealthy in the natural, say you suddenly won millions of dollars from a lottery. How would your life change? I'm pretty sure that we all played with that question in our minds? For me, there would be no more rushing off to work each day. I'd have my own schedule and I would invest my money in a home, so that I would no longer have to pay a mortgage payment. By doing just that alone, I would eliminate one of the biggest toiling of my life. I believe in the spirit realm we too can eliminate the toiling of our lives, when we are no longer grasping and controlling; we can relax and let him do all the work through us. That's complete submission. You can rest from all your work of desperate striving. You will do your best when you give out what God has already put in you to do. Having an undivided heart and an obedient spirit within us, the Father pours out his blessings to restore to us the lost fortunes. God gives every good and perfect gift. Blessings are poured out from the storehouse of the Lord, when we are walking in unity and in alignment to his will. He is wealthy and rich with abundance; we shall lack no good thing. There is rest, prosperity and peace for the soul. We will sit in our rightful place of inheritance and receive our reward. What the enemy meant for our destruction, the Lord fought for us and restored all the treasures the enemy stole from us. The Lord is worthy of our praise. He has fought the battle and won. True Christian victory is not based on our own effort or will-power, but only through grace in Christ Jesus at work in us.

Therefore, we are victorious over-comers through Him alone.

**Psalm 119:162**

> I celebrate because of your promise, like someone who discovers great treasure. (The Voice)

**Hebrews 6:12**

> Imitate those who through faith and patience inherit the promises. (NKJV)

**Malachi 3:10**

> Bring to the storehouse a full tenth of what you earn so there will be food in my house. Test me in this," says the Lord All-Powerful. "I will open the windows of heaven for you and pour out all the blessings you need. (NCV)

**Psalm 41:11**

> I know that you are pleased with me, for my enemy does not triumph over me. (NIV)

**Psalm 23**

> The LORD is my shepherd, I lack nothing. He makes me lie down in green pastures, he leads me beside quiet waters, he refreshes my soul. He guides me along the right paths for his name's sake. Even though I walk through the darkest valley, I will fear no evil, for you are with me; your rod and your

staff, they comfort me. You prepare a table before me in the presence of my enemies. You anoint my head with oil; my cup overflows. Surely your goodness and love will follow me all the days of my life, and I will dwell in the house of the LORD forever. (NIV)

**Isaiah 33:6**

God will be what holds things together, fast and firm during these times. He will be boundless salvation, the roots and fruits of wisdom and knowledge. Zion's most precious possession is the people's awe-filled respect of the Eternal. (Voice)

**Proverbs 8:20-21**

I walk in the way of righteousness, along the paths of justice, bestowing a rich inheritance on those who love me and making their treasuries full. (NIV)

**Colossians 2:2-3**

My goal is that they may be encouraged in heart and united in love, so that they may have the full riches of complete understanding, in order that they may know the mystery of God, namely, Christ, in whom are hidden all the treasures of wisdom and knowledge. (NIV)

**Deuteronomy 29:29**

The secret things belong to the Lord our God, but those things which are revealed belong to us and to our children forever, that we may do all the words of this law. (NKJV)

# Let the Rains Fall Down

Now is the day of reckoning. As we fully surrender our will to His will, the Lord is able to work on our behalf. He defeats our enemies, that habit, that weakness, that circumstance that you were unable to surrender or whatever impossibility that you had. Your Goliath has now been defeated. The Holy Spirit gives you a refreshing burst of power and energy. He fought your battle and claimed your victory. So overjoyed are you, that you could do a victory dance. He now restores all things that the enemy used to destroy you.

Successes and failures help to shape your destiny. After Joseph, who was sold by his brothers into Egypt had suffered for many years in prison, he was made more fruitful and more honorable, than all his brothers. Joseph and his family were allowed to live in the best of all the land. At the end of Job's life, the Lord restored fortune, family and favor, more so, than the first part of Job's life. Naomi, who endured a bitter life of sorrow and experienced one too many deaths, was restored. The Father's love reached out and replaced her emptiness with fullness.

Some of us have endured many sorrows in life, but the father's love has always been to restore us, renew us and revive us. These are the times of refreshing.

**Hebrews 11:32-34**

Do I need to give you more examples? I don't have enough time to tell you about Gideon, Barak, Samson, Jephthah, David, Samuel, and the prophets. All of them had great faith. And with that faith they defeated kingdoms. They did what was right, and God helped them in the ways he promised. With their faith some people closed the mouths of lions. And some were able to stop blazing fires. Others escaped from being killed with swords. Some who were weak were made strong. They became powerful in battle and defeated other armies. (ERV)

**Joel 2:25**

I will restore to you the years that the locust hath eaten. (KJV)

**Jeremiah 30:17**

"For I will restore health to you and heal you of your wounds," says the LORD. (NKJV)

**Psalm 20:5**

And we will shout for joy when you succeed, and we will raise a flag in the name of our God. May the Lord give you all that you ask for. (NCV)

**Psalm 81:10**

I am the LORD your God, who brought you up out of Egypt. Open wide your mouth and I will fill it. (NIV)

**Ezekiel 34:16**

I will search for the lost and bring back the strays. I will bind up the injured and strengthen the weak. (NIV)

**Psalm 86:13**

For Your loyal love for me is so great it is beyond comparison. You have rescued my soul from the depths of the grave. (Voice)

**1 Corinthians 15:55**

O death, where is your victory? Where is your power to hurt?" (ERV)

**Psalm 85:4**

Restore us again, God our Savior, and put away your displeasure toward us. (NIV)

**Psalm 86:11**

Lord, teach me your ways, and I will live and obey your truths. Help me make worshiping your name the most important thing in my life. (ERV)

# The Battle of Kings

Even though, the enemy kings joined forces, the Lord totally subdued and destroyed the enemies of Israel. When the Child puts her trust fully upon the Lord, and will not *take over the wheel*, the Lord will fight her battles, just as he did for the Israelites. In the Spirit realm, we are faced with many battles yet, the King Spirits, Master Spirits and Tyrant Spirits are dethroned and rendered powerless, by the Lord Jesus. The Lord Jesus is invincible in battle! He is always victorious! When we stand in complete faith, we are actually, releasing him to do what he says he would do, and thereby, sweet victory is our reward.

The boundaries, of the Israelite children's inheritance went to the farthest limits, to the sea, to the ravines and to the hill country. The children of God were sent home blessed with riches and plunder from their enemies. They were instructed to share their inheritance with the community and to not rebel or break faith with the Lord any longer.

Our inheritance was already won for us at the cross of calvary, yet we need to claim our rights of inheritance daily by our active faith and to operate in that new realm of victory. As you do, you will gain new areas of spiritual insight.

**Psalm 16:5-6**

The Lord is the portion of my inheritance and my cup; You support my lot. The lines have fallen to me in pleasant places; Indeed, my heritage is beautiful to me. (NASB)

**Isaiah 61:7**

Instead of your shame you will have a double portion, and instead of humiliation they will shout for joy over their portion. Therefore they will possess a double portion in their land, everlasting joy will be theirs. (NASB)

**Psalm 105:44**

He gave them the lands of the nations, and they fell heir to what others had toiled for— (NIV)

**Exodus 15:17**

You will bring them and plant them in the mountain of Your inheritance, The place, O Lord, which You have made for your dwelling, the sanctuary, O Lord, which your hands have established. (NASB)

**Joshua 14:9**

So Moses swore on that day, saying, 'Surely the land on which your foot has trodden will be an inheritance to you and to your children forever, because you have followed the Lord my God fully.' (NASB)

**Isaiah 66:12-14**

This is what the Lord says: "I will give Jerusalem a river of peace and prosperity. The wealth of the nations will flow to her. Her children will be nursed at her breasts, carried in her arms, and held on her lap. I will comfort you there in Jerusalem as a mother comforts her child." When you see these things, your heart will rejoice. You will flourish like the grass! Everyone will see the Lord's hand of blessing on his servants— and his anger against his enemies. (NLT)

# Worship the Lord

Worthy is our King; you are my Kinsmen Redeemer, my Rescuer. Worthy are you our King of Kings, our Rock, our Healer and our Deliver. Worthy are you, our Banner and our Peace. Holy are you, my King. It is well with my soul because my soul longeth after you. Take pleasure in me and the meditations of my heart. I will declare your praises and your marvelous deeds. I will praise you among the people that all might know that the hand of the Lord is powerful and great and that they might always fear the Lord.

**Psalm 111:10**

> Wisdom begins with fear and respect for the Lord. Those who obey him are very wise. Praises will be sung to him forever. (ERV)

**Matthew 6:33**

> We will [shout in] triumph at your salvation and victory, and in the name of our God we will set up our banners. May the Lord fulfill all your petitions. (AMP)

**Psalm 36:5-8**

How precious is your steadfast love, O God! The children of mankind take refuge in the shadow of your wings. They feast on the abundance of your house, and you give them drink from the river of your delights. (ESV)

**Psalm 84:1-2**

How lovely is your dwelling place, LORD Almighty! My soul yearns, even faints, for the courts of the LORD; my heart and my flesh cry out for the living God. (NIV)

# Enter into my Rest

After the children of Israel settled in the land that was promised them an altar was resurrected for the generations to come, not for sacrifice, but to be a witness that the Lord provides and satisfies. Rest too, is our reward. Talk of war was no more and there was sweet rest in the land.

War speaks of the turmoil, yet in His presence is rest. Fully broken and surrendered, you will persevere, yet, cease striving. Only when we are willing to take the risk, to move on from our ordinary and complacent lives, can we experience the level of victory and joy that are in the fullness of Christ Jesus. You must leave the past scars behind to experience a new realm of living. It must be experienced, you can not merely read about it in your doctrine; you must take the journey yourself. This is your story, your witness and your personal testimony.

**1 Peter 1:7**

> These troubles come to prove that your faith is pure. This purity of faith is worth more than gold, which can be proved to be pure by fire but will ruin. But the purity of your faith will bring you praise and glory and honor when Jesus Christ is shown to you. (NCV)

*Gigi Borromeo*

**Colossians 1:12**

He has enabled you to share in the inheritance that belongs to his people, who live in the light. (NLT)

**Matthew 11:28-29**

Come to Me, all you who are weary and heavy-laden, and I will give you rest. Take My yoke upon you and learn from Me, for I am gentle and humble in heart, and you will find rest for your souls. (NASB)

**Jeremiah 30:8**

The Lord All-Powerful says, "At that time I will break the yoke from their necks and tear off the ropes that hold them. Foreign people will never again make my people slaves. (NCV)

**Exodus 33:14**

And the Lord said, My Presence shall go with you, and I will give you rest. (AMP)

**Hebrews 6:10**

For God is not unjust. He will not forget how hard you have worked for him and how you have shown your love to him by caring for other believers, as you still do. (NLT)

174

# New Birth

Where there is fruitfulness in the house of the Lord, there is atmosphere for new birth. A love encounter will bring forth newness of life. A heavenly breakthrough appears like the birth of a child. That which has been long awaited for through much prayer, suddenly comes forth. The righteous cry out and the Lord hears their cry. Once we have learned to know and pursue the heart of God, the Lord then restores our dreams and gives us the desires of our heart.

**Isaiah 66:7-9**

"Before she went into labor, she had the baby. Before the birth pangs hit, she delivered a son. Has anyone ever heard of such a thing? Has anyone seen anything like this? A country born in a day? A nation born in a flash? But Zion was barely in labor when she had her babies! Do I open the womb and not deliver the baby? Do I, the One who delivers babies, shut the womb? (Message)

**1 Samuel 1:20**

And in due time she gave birth to a son. She named him Samuel, for she said, "I asked the Lord for him." (NLT)

**Genesis 21:1-2,6**

Now the LORD was gracious to Sarah as he had said, and the LORD did for Sarah what he had promised. Sarah became pregnant and bore a son to Abraham in his old age, at the very time God had promised him. Sarah said, "God has brought me laughter, and everyone who hears about this will laugh with me." (NIV)

**Luke 1:45-47**

Blessed is she who has believed that the Lord would fulfill his promises to her!" Mary's Song and Mary said: "My soul glorifies the Lord and my spirit rejoices in God my Savior. (NIV)

**Chronicles 4:9**

Now Jabez was more honorable than his brothers, and his mother called his name Jabez, saying, "Because I bore him in pain." And Jabez called on the God of Israel saying, "Oh, that You would bless me indeed, and enlarge my territory, that Your hand would be with me, and that You would keep me from evil, that I may not cause pain!" So God granted him what he requested. (NKJV)

**Proverbs 31:4-6**

> It is not for kings, O Lemuel, it is not for kings to drink wine; nor for princes strong drink: Lest they drink, and forget the law, and pervert the judgment of any of the afflicted. Give strong drink unto him that is ready to perish, and wine unto those that be of heavy hearts. (NLV)

**Isaiah 41:18**

> I will make rivers flow on the dry hills and springs flow through the valleys. I will change the desert into a lake of water and the dry land into fountains of water. (NCV)

**Isaiah 49:10**

> They will not hunger or thirst, nor will the scorching heat or sun strike them down; For He who has compassion on them will lead them and will guide them to springs of water. (NASB)

**Psalm 85:10-12**

> God's love will come together with his faithful people. Goodness and peace will greet them with a kiss. People on earth will be loyal to God, and God in heaven will be good to them. The Lord will give us many good things. The ground will grow many good crops. (ERV)

# When the Lord says, "Shout!"

Children have a special knack for being transparent. They simply can't help but express themselves. Children can be intense and need intense emotional relationships to match their intensity of energy. In my Special Education class, we celebrate every success with elated joy. Children want to express their joy; expression is what children do best. They light up, illuminate, and their souls are transparent.

When I was a child, in my church I saw dancing and leaping in celebration of victory over the enemy or *"spiritual breakthrough,"* as we called it. As you walked in the room you would feel the power and anointing of the Holy Spirit so great it would cause your knees to be weak. Shoes would be kicked off to the side. You would hear crying of every sort: joyful crying, mixed with laughter; childbirth crying, weeping and sometimes wailing. You would hear much celebration and victory. There was laughing that would exhort individuals to dancing and leaping with joy. After an outpouring like this, I asked myself one day, "Lord, are we capable of containing you in these present bodies?" It had seemed too joyous, like being tickled and it making you laugh till it hurt.

Some leaders or ministries will not allow for such an outpouring like this for fear of disorder. Ought children always to be orderly? Remember

David when he danced about in the congregation (2 Samuel 6:16)? David danced with all his heart before the Lord upon the Ark of the Lord returning (2 Samuel 6:14). The trumpets sounded and the people shouted and rejoiced.

David was married to King Saul's daughter Michal. Michal was indignant about David's leaping and dancing. It disturbed her so much, as she thought it was not fitting for a King (2 Samuel 6:20) and the Lord brought judgement upon her.

It is clear to me that the Lord wants rejoicing in his house. When the Father's economy works the way it should, there is call to celebrate. Jesus too rejoiced with his disciples. He had sent seventy-two of them out to proclaim that the Kingdom of God is near and the disciples came back rejoicing that the demons had submitted to them by the authority of the Lord's name, Jesus. They came back with a spiritual rush. Jesus identified with their pleasure, when he said, "I saw Satan fall like lighting from heaven" (Luke 10:18). Jesus celebrates their victory and then took the moment to explain that they had even greater reason to rejoice, that their names are written in heaven. He taught them to base their joy on something far more reliable than accomplishments and abilities. He wanted them to understand that the greatest cause we have for joy is not what we do, but who we are. We are children of the eternal, El Elyon and our names are recorded in heaven. We find joy and confidence, not in what we do because of him, but who we are in him. This understanding of who we are in him is a hidden treasure revealed to us by the Father.

**1 Samuel 4:5**

> And when the ark of the covenant of the Lord came into
> the camp, all Israel shouted so loudly that the earth shook.
> (NKJV)

**John 15:11**

I have told you these things so that you will be filled with my joy. Yes, your joy will overflow! (NLT)

**Psalm 84:5-6**

What joy for those whose strength comes from the Lord, who have set their minds on a pilgrimage to Jerusalem. When they walk through the Valley of Weeping, it will become a place of refreshing springs. The autumn rains will clothe it with blessings. (NLT)

**Luke 10:21**

Then the Holy Spirit made Jesus feel very happy. Jesus said, "I praise you, Father, Lord of heaven and earth. I am thankful that you have hidden these things from those who are so wise and so smart. But you have shown them to people who are like little children. Yes, Father, you did this because it's what you really wanted to do. (ERV)

# Caution to the Wind

The wise and learned of this world are often too sophisticated to throw caution to the wind and release and express their joy, in often undignified manners. If we adult believers refuse to show an ecstatic expression of our emotion of gratitude to our one true love, Jesus Lord of Lords, in the same manner we would over our winning teams, then what message is this saying to our younger believers? When this ecstatic emotion is displayed, it is so unfamiliar to these believers that, they reject and mock their brothers and sisters? More familiar to them are the radical emotions of the world, displaying shouts of elation for sports, or their favorite musicians than for the spiritual. Jesus told us that we had power and authority in his name, through God's Word and His Spirit, to avoid being defeated by the evil one. The problem is we don't always exercise that power. The disciples did in Luke 10 and they were ecstatic! Both Jesus and his disciples were excited over the defeat of the devil.

I'm not saying everyone must do a victory dance, but if you are in this season, you Child, will find a way to express yourself to him in unusual ways. We must dare to do what He is calling us to do! We must follow where He leads. If we always stay in our safe perimeters of sophistication, how will we ever walk by faith, instead of by sight?

This letting go of the rope, so to speak, is what is meant by the expression, "Caution to the wind." It takes trusting in Jesus to act upon a suspicious notion. It takes practice and discipline to sit still and remove the distractions of life far from your mind and concentrate on listening to the Father's voice.

Listening and hearing will then require action. When we act on the request of the Lord, we may at times, like little children error. But if I err, I'd rather err on the side of love. I don't always get it right, but, is it not alright to make a mistake? Are not these the times that the Lord turns into a "teachable moment?" Is he not more proud that we obeyed? It is this hunger for obedience that leads us to our next season - a hunger for holiness.

**1 Corinthians 13:12**

> Now we see things imperfectly, like puzzling reflections in a mirror, but then we will see everything with perfect clarity. All that I know now is partial and incomplete, but then I will know everything completely, just as God now knows me completely. (NLT)

**Psalm 139:3-6**

> You know where I go and where I lie down. You know everything I do. Lord, even before I say a word, you already know it. You are all around me—in front and in back— and have put your hand on me. Your knowledge is amazing to me; it is more than I can understand. (NCV)

**Psalm 139:13-15**

> For you created my inmost being; you knit me together in my mother's womb. I praise you because I am fearfully and wonderfully made; your works are wonderful, I know that

full well. My frame was not hidden from you when I was made in the secret place, when I was woven together in the depths of the earth. (NIV)

**Psalm 78:5-8**

He decreed statutes for Jacob and established the law in Israel, which he commanded our ancestors to teach their children, so the next generation would know them, even the children yet to be born, and they in turn would tell their children. (NIV)

# THE LEADING LADY

### *Winter*

*Winter storms blow your wind,*
*Sound your thunder and roar; have no remorse*
*Wonder of white, though your frost stings like a bitter cup of grief,*
*Your beauty charms, soft and full of peace*
*Your divine light warms us by the fire*
*Release the soul of sorrow*
*Though we labor for winter's food, we need not tire*
*Soaking in the sun, till buds of joy release*
*Oh Silent Night, we say, more and do it again*

# *The Storms*

As Daughters of Heaven, we strive to be His Leading Lady. The Leading Lady is anchored in the foundation of Christ, immovable in faith, fully prepared for the storms of life and equipped with all heavenly culture. She can be sure that the storms of life will come, but she is no longer timid and fearful. She knows that she can do great things. She has mastered current challenges and continues to seek new heights. She knows that she is created for greatness, shaped for success and that she is fearfully and wonderfully made. She will walk in royalty, live in her destiny, and extend her dominion, but never forget to wash the feet of others.

Although, these storms can appear very threatening, the storms are what will get you turned back around and placed right back where you started before you took a turn on the road from your destiny. It is the storms of life that brings back balance in our lives. The storms of life are the challenges that shape us. The storms will realign us with heavens original standard. We read in Luke 8:23 that the disciples were in great danger. "We are going down!" they shouted. Jesus challenged them, "Where is your faith?" The storms will do just that, they will challenge your faith. God allowed the disciples to enter the storm in order that they would experience a supernatural experience like no other. He gave them an experience of power - walking on water.

Be still and experience God!

**Hebrews 6:19**

> This hope is a strong and trustworthy anchor for our souls. It leads us through the curtain into God's inner sanctuary. (NLT)

**Psalm 23:2**

> He leads me beside the still waters. (NKJV)

**Ezekiel 34:25-27**

> "'I'll make a covenant of peace with them. I'll banish fierce animals from the country so the sheep can live safely in the wilderness and sleep in the forest. I'll make them and everything around my hill a blessing. I'll send down plenty of rain in season - showers of blessing! The trees in the orchards will bear fruit, the ground will produce, they'll feel content and safe on their land, and they'll realize that I am God when I break them out of their slavery and rescue them from their slave masters. (MSG)

**Isaiah 41:14-16**

> I will help you. I am the Lord, your Redeemer. I am the Holy One of Israel. You will be a new threshing instrument with many sharp teeth. You will tear your enemies apart, making chaff of mountains. You will toss them into the air, and the wind will blow them all away; a whirlwind will scatter them.

Then you will rejoice in the Lord. You will glory in the Holy One of Israel. (NLT)

**Deuteronomy 33:29**

He is your protecting shield and your triumphant sword! Your enemies will cringe before you, and you will stomp on their backs!" (NLT)

**Isaiah 32:18**

My people will live in peaceful dwelling places, in secure homes, in undisturbed places of rest. (NIV)

# Personal Victory

During a time of transition, our home had sold, when the housing market had shot up so high that we could not find a suitable home in the mountain town that we loved so much. So my family headed to the valley where homes were more affordable. While we had yet to purchase a home, I was waiting on the Lord for direction and insight. Because I had sensed a change coming on in my spirit, I specifically asked the Lord for a sneak preview of the next season of life.

As God was revealing this new season to me, he told me that he was going to educate me and that he wanted me to be a Leading Lady. I wrote that down in the book I was currently reading at the time, *The Leading Lady*, author, T.D. Jakes. This was surely the woman I wanted to be - the Proverbs 31 woman. I had heard about her in many sermons and many Bible Studies. At the moment it seemed inaccessible, unreachable, untouchable - I had no vision for it. I knew that I could not obtain the discipline of this woman's life without a life of holiness. Holiness was what I cowered from. To live a sin-free life seemed like an overwhelming quest. Yet, it is victory over sin in our lives that removes fear. The Lord was asking me to dream big. To see the dream and pull it down from heaven.

Furthering my education was the furtherest thing from my mind, yet two years later, I was enrolled in the local college. If you can remember, I was not a very good student. Not to mention, it had been twenty years since I had graduated from high school. Back when I went to school, the schools did not have the standards they have now. I only learned up to fractions in high school. Of course it didn't help that I moved a lot and I did not attend any one school for any good length of time.

Yet seven years later, from the time I had enrolled in college, I received a bachelor's degree in Liberal Studies. Neither of my parents had graduated from Junior High-School. No one understands the personal victory it meant for me to receive a degree. Overcoming my educational gap was only one of the longings of my heart, but somehow the Lord was positioning me to gain, not only more knowledge, but more wisdom. Winning this one personal victory set me on a path to know my true destiny.

God groomed David, a shepherd boy to be a King and he too is grooming you and I. He has been grooming us for the ministry of his Gospel. To be teachers of his Word and to love all people and bless others, this includes your enemies. This is Christ-living, holy and acceptable, godliness and the high calling of us all.

**Psalm 90:12**

> Oh! Teach us to live well! Teach us to live wisely and well! (MSG)

**Psalm 90:17**

> Let the favor of the Lord our God be upon us, and establish the work of our hands upon us; yes, establish the work of our hands! (ESV)

**Psalm 86:11-12**

Lord, teach me what you want me to do, and I will live by your truth. Teach me to respect you completely. Lord, my God, I will praise you with all my heart, and I will honor your name forever. (NCV)

**Deuteronomy 32:2**

My teachings will come like the rain, like a mist falling to the ground, like a gentle rain on the soft grass, like rain on the green plants. (ERV)

**Luke 1:45**

Blessed is she who has believed that the Lord would fulfill his promises to her!" (NIV)

# Building the Home

King David had in his heart to build the Lord a house, a place for the ark of the covenant to rest upon. A curtain was to surround the ark and separate the holy place from the most holy place. There in the most holy place the Lord's presence would meet and commune with the leaders of Israel, the priest. The lamps must burn continually before the Lord. The tablets of the Law were placed in the ark. The Lord desires to make his home in us and his law to be written in our hearts. The foundation and root system of our life is that internal world, where nobody sees. It is developed in secret and in private. God will establish a strong and healthy foundation in order for you to bear fruit that he has called you to bear. When we try on our own to build our house of religion it will often fail. When things are falling apart the Lord often tears down the old in order to build up the new. The home I built did not stand the storm; it crumbled in 2011. In March of 2012, my husband of 15 years served me divorce papers. The family we had established, now live in two separate homes.

However a home for the Lord must be undefiled. The Leading Lady must live in an unbroken fellowship with Christ Jesus, the Lord. She must learn to pursue and step into God's presence daily. The Lord will show us how to live in true freedom. True freedom is life unbound of sin and strife. When you are hungry enough to not want for just an ordinary life you will hunger for his holiness. When all we want in life is to live for him only and bring others to his saving grace, the Lord reveals his will to us. The Lord will build the house; she will be a strong house.

**Psalm 24:7**

> Lift up your heads, O gates, and be lifted up, O ancient doors, that the King of glory may come in! (NASB)

**1 Peter 2:5**

> You also, as living stones, are being built into a spiritual house, a holy priesthood, to offer up spiritual sacrifices acceptable to God through Jesus Christ. (NKJV)

**Acts 24:16**

> Therefore I do my best always to have a clear conscience toward God and all people. (NRSV)

**1 Chronicles 17:12**

> He shall build a house for me, and I will establish his throne forever. (ESV)

**Luke 6:48**

> That person is like a man building a house who dug deep and laid the foundation on rock. When the floods came, the water tried to wash the house away, but it could not shake it, because the house was built well. (NCV)

**Isaiah 54:11-12**

"O storm-battered city, troubled and desolate! I will rebuild you with precious jewels and make your foundations from lapis lazuli. I will make your towers of sparkling rubies, your gates of shining gems, and your walls of precious stones. (NLT)

**Acts 4:11**

Jesus is "'the stone you builders rejected, which has become the cornerstone.' (NIV)

**Hebrews 3:4-6**

For every house has a builder, but the one who built everything is God. Moses was certainly faithful in God's house as a servant. His work was an illustration of the truths God would reveal later. But Christ, as the Son, is in charge of God's entire house. And we are God's house, if we keep our courage and remain confident in our hope in Christ. (NLT)

**1 Corinthians 3:16**

Do you not know that you are a temple of God and that the Spirit of God dwells in you? (NASB)

**Exodus 15:17**

You will lead your people and place them on your very own mountain, the place that you, Lord, made for yourself to live, the temple, Lord, that your hands have made. (NCV)

# Holy Mountain

Winter weather can be bitter cold and uncomfortable. Higher faith will be required to bare the winter storms, vigorous as they are, the Leading Lady has prepared for the winter - no longer intimidated, fearful and afraid of change. No longer is she embittered by the pains of life. The Leading Lady will bear up under anything and everything that comes her way without weakening or complaining. She has learned the discipline of making still her mouth. It is in the stillness, that she hears his call.

Deep in the wilderness is the mountain. In a desperate cry for holiness she follows him up the mountain of transformation. Upward, with each stride, she will climb the mountain of her faith. Exercising every spiritual muscle of her body until it burns a satisfying burn. On the mountaintop you will encounter God. Using royal lenses you will see an aerial view and gain a new perspective of your identity. You will see life from a limitless perspective. You too, will hear the voice of God and when you listen in the silence, you can hear his heart beat. The Lord and his heart becomes her passion and one desire. The storm brings order like a perfect snowflake.

I once feared being holy. I mostly feared being accepted by others. I feared how I might talk, what I might look like and what strange things the Lord may ask of me. I've heard the stories of the missionaries. I know the story of the prophets. The children of Israel too, were frightened of God's holiness. They asked for Moses to put a veil over his face because the light of the Lord's glory shown brightly. But you Leading Lady must shine. In his presence is immense healing powers. He is a God who heals. He heals broken bodies, broken minds, broken hearts, broken lives and broken relationships. He renews your thinking and your negative mindset. He makes all things whole. We find inner healing in his presence, so that we can reach out externally to others. Unless we have our own inner healing, we cannot love others exponentially as we should.

**2 Corinthians 3:13**

> We are not like Moses, who put a veil over his face so the people of Israel would not see the glory. (NLT)

**Psalm 42:1-2**

> As the deer pants for streams of water, so my soul pants for you, my God. My soul thirsts for God, for the living God. When can I go and meet with God? (NIV)

**Psalm 24:3-4**

> Who may climb the mountain of the Lord? Who may stand in his holy place? Only those whose hands and hearts are pure, who do not worship idols and never tell lies. (NLT)

**Isaiah 57:13**

> But those taking refuge in me will inherit the land and possess my holy mountain. (CEB)

**John 14:27**

Peace I leave with you; my peace I give you. I do not give to you as the world gives. Do not let your hearts be troubled and do not be afraid. (NIV)

**Jeremiah 33:11**

There will be sounds of joy and happiness. There will be the happy sounds of a bride and groom. There will be the sounds of people bringing their gifts to the Lord's Temple. They will say, 'Praise the Lord All- Powerful! The Lord is good! His faithful love will last forever!' They will say this because I will again do good things to Judah. It will be as it was in the beginning." This is what the Lord said. (ERV)

# Ascending the Mountain

It is upon the mountaintop experience that you truly realize that you most certainly can live a sin-free life; no longer bound by sin and condemnation. Sin is dealt with expediently, as God has already made provision for your sin. We being born of God, the Righteous, we desire with passion to be as he is. We were created in his image. God came in the flesh to look like us so that we could look like him. We live not as the world, but as citizens of our true home. We are citizens of heaven. It is his Holy Spirit that empowers us to live a sin-free life. In fact, it is our destiny.

When you are loving and enjoying the Lord there is no need for the law. The law is merely for them who have no heart to walk in the Spirit, who do not obey God and who are still entangled in the affairs of this world. Our father has put a new law in our hearts. As a daughter of the most High God, whose throne it is in heaven and whose footstool is upon the earth, your greatest desire is to experience the Kingdom and please him. He the Lord, has been graciously awaiting that you would follow in his footsteps and understand your calling. We were designed to live in the authority and dominion of our father, ruling and reigning as royalty. We must rule over sin and subdue it. Sin must be dealt with moment by moment. Where the spirit of truth rules, you will actually find effortless victory, because sin will no longer have a grip on you. Although we are in a perpetual state of warfare and constantly aware of our inadequacy, Christ has given us the authority to live a victorious life.

**Exodus 3:5**

> "Take off your sandals, for you are standing on holy ground. (NLT)

**1 John 3:9**

> No one born of God makes a practice of sinning, for God's seed abides in him, and he cannot keep on sinning because he has been born of God. (ESV)

**Jude 1:24**

> God is strong and can keep you from falling. He can bring you before his glory without any wrong in you and give you great joy. (ERV)

**2 Timothy 2:24**

> And the servant of the Lord must not strive; but be gentle unto all men, apt to teach, patient. (KJV)

**Colossians 2:9-10**

> For in Him dwells all the fulness of the Godhead bodily; and you are complete in Him, who is the head of all principality and power. (NKJV)

**Titus 3:5**

He saved us, not because of the righteous things we had done, but because of his mercy. He washed away our sins, giving us a new birth and new life through the Holy Spirit. (NLT)

**Romans 6:6-7**

For we know that our old self was crucified with him so that the body ruled by sin might be done away with, that we should no longer be slaves to sin — because anyone who has died has been set free from sin. (NIV)

**Romans 6:22**

But now being made free from sin, and become servants to God, ye have your fruit unto holiness, and the end everlasting life. (KJV)

**Romans 6:14**

For sin shall not have dominion over you, for you are not under law but under grace. (NKJV)

**1 Peter 4:1**

Therefore, since Christ suffered in his body, arm yourselves also with the same attitude, because whoever suffers in the body is done with sin. (NIV)

**1 Corinthians 15:24-25**

Then comes the end, when he delivers the kingdom to God the Father after destroying every rule and every authority and power. For he must reign until he has put all his enemies under his feet. (ESV)

**Isaiah 40:9**

Get thee up into the high mountain; O Jerusalem, that bringest good tidings, lift up thy voice with strength; lift it up, be not afraid; say unto the cities of Judah, Behold your God! (KJV)

**Isaiah 55:10-13**

"Rain and snow fall from the sky and don't return until they have watered the ground. Then the ground causes the plants to sprout and grow, and they produce seeds for the farmer and food for people to eat. In the same way, my words leave my mouth, and they don't come back without results. My words make the things happen that I want to happen. They succeed in doing what I send them to do. "So you will go out from there with joy. You will be led out in peace. When you come to the mountains and hills, they will begin singing. All the trees in the fields will clap their hands. Large cypress trees will grow where there were thorn bushes. Myrtle trees will grow where there were weeds. All this will happen to make the Lord known, to be a permanent reminder of his goodness and power." (ERV)

# A Burning Bush

On the mountaintop, Moses received his high calling. In his presence, God reveals his heart. Being strengthened in faith, greatness will cry out to you. Every woman of destiny has a high calling. Her first calling is to godly living and personal discipline. She has a high calling to love her husband and children then, to love others, but when she has learned to have compassion for the lost, lonely and downtrodden, she has touched the very heart of God. Christ Jesus the Lord came to set humanity free. If we are to be as Christ is, then we too, are going to have a heart for the lost; to bring hope to the hopeless. It is easy to love the ones that return our love, but it takes a supernatural love to love them, who prove difficult to love by human standards. Going outside of our comfort zone is going to take wings to fly.

When Moses went to the Lord's Holy mountain he questioned his ability to be used before God, but God made Moses a great leader among the people of Israel. Like Moses, God is calling you to lead his people out of captivity. It is a high calling. It is his heart.

**Psalm 83:14-15**

As fire consumes the forest or a flame sets the mountains ablaze, so pursue them with your tempest and terrify them with your storm. (NIV)

**Isaiah 61:1**

The Spirit of the Lord God is upon me, because the Lord has anointed me to bring good news to the afflicted; he has sent me to bind up the brokenhearted, to proclaim liberty to captives and freedom to prisoners. (NASB)

**John 3:16**

For God loved the world so much that he gave his one and only Son, so that everyone who believes in him will not perish but have eternal life. (NLT)

**Psalm 68:5**

A father of the fatherless, a defender of widows, Is God in His holy habitation. (ESV)

**James 1:27**

Pure and undefiled religion in the sight of our God and Father is this: to visit orphans and widows in their distress, and to keep oneself unstained by the world. (NASB)

**Colossians 3:12-14**

God loves you and has chosen you as his own special people. So be gentle, kind, humble, meek, and patient. Put up with each other, and forgive anyone who does you wrong, just as Christ has forgiven you. Love is more important than anything else. It is what ties everything completely together. (CEV)

**Ruth 3:11**

And now, my daughter, don't be afraid. I will do for you all you ask. All the people of my town know that you are a woman of noble character. (NIV)

**Matthew 28:19-20**

Therefore, go and make disciples of all nations, baptizing them in the name of the Father and of the Son and of the Holy Spirit, teaching them to obey everything that I've commanded you. Look, I myself will be with you every day until the end of this present age." (CEB)

**Romans 12:7**

If your gift is serving others, serve them well. If you are a teacher, teach well. (NLT)

**John 8:15**

You judge me the way people judge other people. I don't judge anyone. (ERV)

# In His Presence

When Moses went to the see the burning bush, who was on the Lord's mind? Yes, the children of Israel. The Lord was concerned for their suffering. He heard their cry and he had compassion on them. He shared with Moses that he would rescue them from their oppressor and Moses would be the instrument he, the Lord would use. Then the Lord told Moses, when he has delivered them out of their bondage, they will worship Him at the mountain. The mountain is a place of deep worship and communing. You will sit and learn what it is to be a daughter of the King of Kings. It is on the mountaintop that we experience a special encounter with Him. We encounter his Holiness. Holiness is an experience; it is not a religion. It is that place of deep intimacy that brings oneness. Holiness is a standard; it means whole or complete. Holiness is transforming all your thoughts to filter through the mind of God. Holiness is the exact contrast to sin. It causes us to take control of our thoughts and bring them immediately under subjection and no longer following their usual pattern. By living in this holy discipline we are empowered to live in a way that reflects his love and power. When you are able to live this way, effortlessly, without work and condemnation, you have found true freedom. Because remember we were once slaves to sin.

As you wait for his glory to fall down and set your heart on fire, you will encounter his presence. Here in His presence, everything bows to the King of Kings. In His presence heaven and earth become one. The Lord will establish his favor and anointing. In the light of his presence, when his face shines upon you, there is joy and strength for your soul. The nutrients of the Father's love will enhance your growth. With new revelation, a new dream emerges, a dream for life, to live and truly live the abundant and fullness of life.

It is when we hunger for his holiness that we head for the mountain. Spiritual hunger will cause people to dream. Hunger is the motivating factor to move out of ourselves, out of our comfort and convenience. When we've pressed on to the higher planes, we change our perspective about our ability to be used. The voice of the hungry will cry out to impact the destinies of people and cities. It is the hungry who establish the city and change the system and the structures. Hunger will pull down on heaven until heaven becomes your environment - your heavenly culture. We were created for Kingdom works. We walk in royalty to transact Kingdom business and to advance the Kingdom. We were empowered to take dominion over our circumstances and change our environment. Like Peter who stepped out of the boat, Peter knew that he could imitate Christ and walk on water. Walking in our dominion will command purposeful living. We will walk in freedom and stretch and extend our full potential to the point of discomfort. We will spiritually labor until greatness is released; this is a great pressing in, as in the woman who came to Jesus with an issue of blood. No longer fearful of the enemy and no longer afraid of pain, the Leading Lady will subdue and inspire others to do so as well.

**Psalm 63:2**

> I have seen your power and your glory in the place of worship. (CEV)

**Exodus 33:11**

So the Lord spoke to Moses face to face, as a man speaks to his friend. (NKJV)

**Romans 6:13**

Do not present your members to sin as instruments for unrighteousness, but present yourselves to God as those who have been brought from death to life, and your members to God as instruments for righteousness. (ESV)

**Micah 4:1-2**

It shall come to pass in the latter days that the mountain of the house of the Lord shall be established as the highest of the mountains, and it shall be lifted up above the hills; and peoples shall flow to it, and many nations shall come, and say: "Come, let us go up to the mountain of the Lord, to the house of the God of Jacob, that he may teach us his ways and that we may walk in his paths." For out of Zion shall go forth the law, and the word of the Lord from Jerusalem. (ESV)

**Hebrews 12:26-29**

When God spoke from Mount Sinai his voice shook the earth, but now he makes another promise: "Once again I will shake not only the earth but the heavens also." This means that all of creation will be shaken and removed, so that only unshakable things will remain. Since we are receiving a Kingdom that is unshakable, let us be thankful and please God by worshiping him with holy fear and awe. For our God is a devouring fire. (NLT)

**John 4:23**

But the hour is coming, and is now here, when the true worshipers will worship the Father in spirit and truth, for the Father seeks such as these to worship him. (NRSV)

**John 17:22-23**

The glory that you have given me I have given to them, that they may be one even as we are one, I in them and you in me, that they may become perfectly one, so that the world may know that you sent me and loved them even as you loved me. (ESV)

**Matthew 6:10**

May your kingdom come and what you want be done, here on earth as it is in heaven. (NCV)

# Prepare for Expansion

As you encounter his sweet spirit, He will reestablish his house - the temple, that is in you. You will soak in all of his goodness and light. You will fall in love with your first love all over again. You will host his very presence. The light of the Lord's presence is where your strength will come from. There you will warm up to his embrace and realize his unlimited resources. His passion will burn in you. You will find unshakeable faith and develop a praise language. Being in awe of His awesome wonder, you will go anywhere he wants, say anything he wants or do anything he asks, because you are completely His. A holy boldness now comes upon you. You are in his fullness. With boldness, you will find you can come to His throne and ask whatever you will. The Leading Lady is now equipped with her new assignment to advance the kingdom. She is anointed to be a minister of God and to rebuild cities.

No longer is she willing to live the ordinary life. She was once afraid to ask for the impossible, *the miracles*, to expect more. With holy boldness, power and authority, she will speak to the mountains and tell them to move and they will move. For when we move the mountain we only have the hills to contend with. Now, willing to take risks, pursuit of His presence becomes her daily quest. Before a day has a chance to go awry, place the wood on the altar of praise. Choose intimacy everyday, because erosion begins with neglect. You must keep the wood on the altar in order to keep the fire burning, in order to stay in alignment with the will of God. You will be ignited to release this holy, passion within.

**Psalm 119:147-148**

> I rise before dawn and cry for help; I hope in thy words. (RSV)

**Psalm 90:14**

> Satisfy us each morning with your unfailing love, so we may sing for joy to the end of our lives. (NLT)

**Psalm 84:11**

> For the Lord God is a Sun and Shield; the Lord bestows [present] grace *and* favor and [future] glory (honor, splendor, and heavenly bliss)! No good thing will He withhold from those who walk uprightly. (AMP)

**Psalm 89:15**

> Happy are the people who know how to praise you. Lord, let them live in the light of your presence. (NCV)

**Exodus 15:13**

> "With your unfailing love you lead the people you have redeemed. In your might, you guide them to your sacred home. (NLT)

**1 Chronicles 16:11-12**

> Seek the Lord and his strength; seek his presence continually! Remember the wondrous works that he has done, his miracles and the judgments he uttered. (ESV)

**Ephesians 4:24**

> You learned Christ! My assumption is that you have paid careful attention to him, been well instructed in the truth precisely as we have it in Jesus. Since, then, we do not have the excuse of ignorance, everything — and I do mean everything—connected with that old way of life has to go. It's rotten through and through. Get rid of it! And then take on an entirely new way of life—a God-fashioned life, a life renewed from the inside and working itself into your conduct as God accurately reproduces his character in you. (Message)

**Hebrews 13:15**

> Therefore, let us continually offer to God a sacrifice of praise—the fruit of lips that openly profess his name. (NIV)

# *Daughters of Destiny*

As a princess-daughter we will be sent as representatives of the King of Kings, to be used as an instrument for his righteousness and to admonish the needs of others. When the Leading Lady has encountered that which is in heaven, she will bring the father's love to the earth. The Leading Lady is gracious in speech, pleasant and seasoned with salt and speaks the truth. Knowing that the father loves all his creation, the *Leading Lady* honors all people. When we know who we are, we begin to think right, talk right, and act right. She will be willing to give up anything and laying it all down for Christ sake. You will be saying, "Use me Lord for your Glory!" When you find out who God has you to be, you will never want to be anyone else. Daughters of Heaven, get a glimpse of your royal destiny. Ask the Lord to show you his purpose for which you were created for. Ask him to show you what you are passionate about. For you were born with purpose. As representatives, we will walk victoriously as conquerors and we will represent the King well.

**Isaiah 60:1**

> Arise, shine; For your light has come! And the glory of the LORD is risen upon you. (NIV)

213

**Revelation 5:10**

> You made them to be a kingdom of priests for our God, and they will rule on the earth." (NCV)

**2 Corinthians 5:20**

> Therefore, we are ambassadors for Christ, as though God were making an appeal through us; we beg you on behalf of Christ, be reconciled to God. (NASB)

**Proverbs 4:5-7**

> Get wisdom; get insight; do not forget, and do not turn away from the words of my mouth. Do not forsake her, and she will keep you; love her, and she will guard you. The beginning of wisdom is this: Get wisdom, and whatever you get, get insight. (ESV)

**Proverbs 20:15**

> Gold there is, and rubies in abundance, but lips that speak knowledge are a rare jewel. (NIV)

**Isaiah 61:1**

> The Lord God's spirit is upon me, because the Lord has anointed me. He has sent me to bring good news to the poor, to bind up the brokenhearted, to proclaim release for captives, and liberation for prisoners. (CEB)

# *Rule and Reign*

To call forth heaven's culture to the Earth, as it was in the garden before the fall, is to rule and reign in the Father's interest. To be in perfect union with the Lord's mind is to call heaven to earth to promote his glory throughout the earth.

When we are empowered by his Spirit, we are happy, creative, innovative and walking in freedom. Lives can't help but be supernaturally drawn to us by divine appointment. People need to know what hope we have for them. People are hungry to experience the goodness of the Lord. Our life of abundance is our testimony. The Leading Lady will display the Lord's righteousness and his glory with a new and fresh revelation. Her life and reputation will bring honor to the King of Glory. She will navigate life well.

**1 Timothy 2:1-4**

> First, I tell you to pray for all people, asking God for what they need and being thankful to him. Pray for rulers and for all who have authority so that we can have quiet and peaceful lives full of worship and respect for God. This is

good, and it pleases God our Savior, who wants all people to be saved and to know the truth. (NCV)

**Mark 16:18**

They will be able to place their hands on the sick, and they will be healed." (NLT)

**Philippians 4:13**

I can be content in any and every situation through the Anointed One who is my power and strength. (Voice)

**Revelation 12:11**

And they overcame him by the blood of the Lamb and by the word of their testimony, and they did not love their lives to the death. (NKJV)

**1 Thessalonians 4:11-12**

Do all you can to live a peaceful life. Mind your own business, and earn your own living, as we told you before. If you do these things, then those who are not believers will respect the way you live. And you will not have to depend on others for what you need. (ERV)

**Colossians 3:14**

But above all these things put on love, which is the bond of perfection. (NKJV)

**1 Thessalonians 4:1**

Finally then, brethren, we request and exhort you in the Lord Jesus, that as you received from us instruction as to how you ought to walk and please God (just as you actually do walk), that you excel still more. (NASB)

# A Planting of the Lord

When an olive tree is young it needs a stake to hold it upright, but once the trunk is stronger, it no longer requires the stake for holding. When you are the *Child* you will need the father's hand and sheltering, but when you have matured and are *strong* and know how to bare the storms, the father can let go of the hand, with the promise that he will always be there. He is fully confident that we will do well. We were once disciples learning to follow in the Lord's footsteps, yet now, like an apostle, you are being sent. You are being sent to the world to produce a harvest. Your life is a fruitful vine, interwoven and touching many lives. You cannot be uprooted or disconnected from the vine. You are a planting of the Lord, made to be fruitful. You are meant to be thriving and successful. You will stand upright. You will stand strong, even when the storms blow. You will have a fiery passion for the right things and a greater desire for sacrifice. You will flourish in many meaningful relationships, although, because of the enemy, you will pay a price to sustain them. Fellowship will be a sacrifice, because the enemy wants to destroy relationships. For when you desire to be in the likeness of Jesus we are often misunderstood.

But you will build up the body of believers and share the inheritance, blessings and giving freely. You will handle the torrential storms and you will take on greater works of service and responsibility. For you are a planting of the Lord, rooted and grounded - you are strong and mighty in the Lord.

**Psalm 52:8-9**

> But I am like an olive tree, thriving in the house of God. I will always trust in God's unfailing love. I will praise you forever, O God, for what you have done. I will trust in your good name in the presence of your faithful people. (NLT)

**Psalm 92:12-14**

> Good people will prosper like palm trees, and they will grow strong like the cedars of Lebanon. They will take root in your house, Lord God, and they will do well. They will be like trees that stay healthy and fruitful, even when they are old. (CEV)

**Isaiah 61:3-4**

> They will be called oaks of righteousness, a planting of the Lord for the display of his splendor. They will rebuild the ancient ruins and restore the places long devastated; they will renew the ruined cities that have been devastated for generations. (NIV)

**Ephesians 4:12-13**

> Prepare God's people for works of service, so that the body of Christ may be built up until we all reach unity in the faith and in the knowledge of the Son of God and become mature, attaining to the whole measure of the fullness of Christ. (NIV1984)

**2 Corinthians 8:7**

> You are rich in everything—in faith, in speaking ability, in knowledge, in the willingness to help, and in the love you learned from us. So now we want you to be rich in this work of giving too. (ERV)

**Colossians 1:12**

> Giving thanks to the Father, who has qualified and made us fit to share the portion which is the inheritance of the saints (God's holy people) in the Light. (AMP)

**2 Chronicles 31:5**

> As soon as the king's command went out to the Israelites, they gave freely of the first portion of their grain, new wine, oil, honey, and everything they grew in their fields. They brought a large amount, one-tenth of everything. (NCV)

**Proverbs 3:9-10**

> Honor the Lord with your wealth and with the first of all your crops. Then your barns will be filled with plenty, and your vats will burst with wine. (CEB)

# The Lesson in the Storm

Why would we be sent into the fiercest of storms? To connect with whatever we unsuccessfully were not able to connect with in previous times - to actually experience what you know to be true, but were unable to successfully overcome.

Anyone who wants to live a holy life in Christ Jesus will experience a spiritual persecution. Although blessed and lacking no good thing, we still momentarily go through times of great pain. But how we will suffer through persecution is different, because we know our identity and purpose. Because we are steadfast and single-minded, we will not be moved. No more cowering down in fear to the enemy. We stand firm in our pursuit of righteousness, faith, love and peace.

Once you have spent time communing in his inner sanctuary, knowing him, loving him and worshipping him, two things will happen: You will eternally praise him and you will love people senseless. The realization that God truly loves each one of us, in the whole world and - not just the Saints, but all mankind - gives us a sense of brotherhood, a compassion for souls and a dignity for mankind.

**2 Corinthians 2:14**

But thank God, who is always leading us around through Christ as if we were in a parade. He releases the fragrance of the knowledge of him everywhere through us. (CEB)

**John 5:36**

"But I have a proof about myself that is greater than anything John said. The things I do are my proof. These are what my Father gave me to do. They show that the Father sent me. (ERV)

**1 Timothy 3:7**

And he must have a good reputation with those outside the church, so that he will not fall into reproach and the snare of the devil. (NASB)

**Psalm 71:17-18**

You have taught me since I was young, O God, and I still proclaim the wonderful things You have done. Now as I grow old and my hair turns gray, I ask that You not abandon me, O God. Allow me to share with the generation to come about your power; let me speak about your strength and wonders to all those yet to be born. (VOICE)

**Hebrews 13:3-5**

Remember those in prison, as if you were there yourself. Remember also those being mistreated, as if you felt their pain in your own bodies. Give honor to marriage, and remain faithful to one another in marriage. God will surely judge people who are immoral and those who commit adultery. Don't love money; be satisfied with what you have. For God has said, "I will never fail you. I will never abandon you." (NLT)

# *Washing the Feet of Others*

I tried emotionally preparing for Mother's day, since it was not predictable whether my last two children would be spending the day with me. My two children no longer physically live with me. They live with their father. In preparation for Mother's day, I decided I would honor two mother's randomly, who I would not know. I decided in my heart that I would not allow myself a victim's mindset of self pity. I prepared in advance that I would be a blessing instead. I sought out these mothers by driving through town. After praying and asking God who he would want to bless and honor, he highlighted two moms. One mother walked with her son on the street. I pulled over to her in my car and when I spoke to her it looked as though her son may have been specially challenged. I was pleased to show the Father's love and gift her. The other woman was across town and had four small children and the youngest, she strolled in the stroller. Like the other woman, I pulled to the side and decided I would bless her as well. To be able to lift the human spirit is rewarding beyond measure. It is now my desire to make this a Mother's Day tradition.

With renewed compassion for souls, we begin to see people as he sees them. With fear banished, you will respond to the needs of others, without excuse and with pure generosity. When we experience the heart of another, we will treat people with dignity and honor. We will feel what they feel. We will not only intercede for them, but take action for them, giving, pouring, serving and visiting. Our arms extended, reaching, we no longer hide, we shine!

**Exodus 16:4**

> Then the LORD said to Moses, "I will rain down bread from heaven for you. The people are to go out each day and gather enough for that day. In this way I will test them and see whether they will follow my instructions. (NIV)

**John 4:36**

> The harvesters are paid good wages, and the fruit they harvest is people brought to eternal life. What joy awaits both the planter and the harvester alike! (NLT)

**John 5:17**

> Jesus replied, "My Father is still working, and I am working too." (CEB)

**2 Corinthians 9:9-11**

> As it is written,"He scattered abroad, he gave to the poor, His righteousness endures forever." Now He who supplies seed to the sower and bread for food will supply and multiply your seed for sowing and increase the harvest of your righteousness; you will be enriched in everything for all liberality, which through us is producing thanksgiving to God. (NASB)

**1 Peter 4:10**

Use whatever gift you've received for the good of one another so that you can show yourselves to be good stewards of God's grace in all its varieties. (VOICE)

**Psalm 82:3-4**

Defend the weak and the orphans; defend the rights of the poor and suffering. Save the weak and helpless; free them from the power of the wicked. (NCV)

# Rain Falls Down

Holy rain is released from heaven, like manna, when we show true stewardship toward the Kingdom of God. Stewardship of the blessings of God's hidden powers are essential to maintaining possession of the inheritance. God's promise for plentifulness is evident that he desires that the work be done again and more of it. The believer's obedience to follow God allows God to breakthrough to invade Earth with a supernatural outpouring. With joy we begin to see impossibilities and problems bend their knees to the name of Jesus Christ, like our cities being transformed.

Thereby ministering to the Lord, we are strengthen and empowered. We operate in the overflow and outgrowth of our filled spirit; we will actually partner with heaven. God specializes in things thought impossible. For it is when you begin to understand the Kingdom that you begin to demonstrate it. Until you encounter that which is thought impossible, you never truly experience your true identity. What an amazing journey!

**Leviticus 26:4**

I will give you rains at the right season; the land will produce crops, and the trees of the field will produce their fruit. (NCV)

**1 Corinthians 4:1-2**

People should think of us as servants of Christ, the ones God has trusted with his secrets. Now in this way those who are trusted with something valuable must show they are worthy of that trust. (NCV)

**Deuteronomy 28:12**

The Lord shall open unto thee his good treasure, the heaven to give the rain unto thy land in his season, and to bless all the work of thine hand: and thou shalt lend unto many nations, and thou shalt not borrow. (KJV)

**Deuteronomy 8:18**

"And you shall remember the Lord your God, for it is He who gives you power to get wealth, that He may establish His covenant which He swore to your fathers, as it is this day. (NKJV)

**John 14:12-13**

"I tell you the truth, anyone who believes in me will do the same works I have done, and even greater works, because I am going to be with the Father. You can ask for anything in my name, and I will do it, so that the Son can bring glory to the Father. (NLT)

**Isaiah 62:11**

Behold, the Lord has proclaimed to the end of the earth: Say to the daughter of Zion, "Behold, your salvation comes; behold, his reward is with him, and his recompense before him." (RSV)

# Ascribe to the Lord

*Holy, Holy, our you Lord. You abound in goodness. I exalt you, Lord on high. Worthy are you of all praise. Praise you Lord for the storm. May everything I do, please you. Everything I have is not my own, but it is for you. You have my heart, my soul, my life; you have it all! You shower me with blessings. You thought me how to dream. Thank you for the plentifulness Lord. You love me! You want for my success! So great and wonderful is the Lord my God. Your compassion and faithfulness is everlasting. There is no God like you. I love you! I am satisfied in you. I have no other want or need. You have supplied all my need. Therefore you are everything I need. You are the strength of my life. Because I am free and because I am loved, I will tell the world. You are worthy! I will shout! I will sing of your glory forever.*

**Isaiah 62:1**

> For Zion's sake I will not keep silent, and for Jerusalem's sake I will not keep quiet, until her righteousness goes forth like brightness, and her salvation like a torch that is burning. (NASB)

**Isaiah 61:10**

I am filled with joy and my soul vibrates with exuberant hope, because of the Eternal my God; For He has dressed me with the garment of salvation, wrapped me with the robe of righteousness. It's as though I'm dressed for my wedding day, in the very best: a bridegroom's garland and a bride's jewels. (VOICE)

**1 Chronicles 16:28-36**

Praise the Lord, all people of every nation; praise the Lord's glory and power! Give the Lord praise worthy of his glory. Come into his presence with your offerings. Worship the Lord in all his holy beauty. Everyone on earth should tremble before him! But the world stands firm and cannot be moved. Let the heavens rejoice and the earth be happy! Let people everywhere say, "The Lord rules!" Let the sea and everything in it shout for joy! Let the fields and everything in them be happy! The trees of the forest will sing for joy when they see the Lord, because he is coming to rule the world. Give thanks to the Lord because he is good. His faithful love will last forever. Say to him, "Save us, God our Savior. Bring us back together, and save us from the other nations. Then we will give thanks to your holy name and joyfully praise you." Praise the Lord, the God of Israel! He always was and will always be worthy of praise!

All the people praised the Lord and said "Amen!" (ERV)